CREATIVE SEQUENCE

Teaching Music

with Flexibility *and* Organization

by Tim Purdum

Published by

Creative Sequence
Teaching Music with Flexibility and Organization

by
Tim Purdum

© 2012 by Tim Purdum

Cover illustration and design by Benjamin Hitmar. © 2012 by Tim Purdum.
Photographs © 2012 by Carole Fishback. Used by permission.
Images of children in this book were used with the express written permission of their parents.

Purchase of this book gives the user access to restricted pages on
cs.cedarrivermusic.com, and permission to photocopy charts and tables
for use in teaching children. All other rights reserved.
For permission requests, contact the author.

Cedar River Music
2304 Franklin Street
Cedar Falls, IA 50613
www.cedarrivermusic.com
tim@cedarrivermusic.com

Printed in the United States of America

ISBN 978-0-9859001-0-6

First Edition, 2012

Acknowledgements

As with any new endeavor in our digital age, I stand upon the shoulders of giants as I write. The giants in music education include Carl Orff and Gunild Keetman, whose vision of creative, playful movement and music have inspired generations, and Zoltan Kodály, who foresaw the need to collect the world's treasures of folk music, and share this with our children. I owe a huge debt of gratitude to my personal mentors in the Orff Schulwerk: JoElla Hug, Roger Sams, Sofia López-Ibor, James Harding, Brian Burnett, Maggie Hoffee, Arvida Steen, Jay Broeker, and Steven Calantropio. Much of what you see in these pages is inspired by these great educators.

Thank you to my sister-in-law, Julia Bullard, for her editing, suggestions, and encouragement. Thanks also to my father, Alan Purdum, who in addition to editing, has always been the role model for my life and career.

And finally, thank you to Suzanne and Elliot, my family. Without the support that Suzanne gives me every day, I would not be able to tackle projects such as this. My hope is that ***Creative Sequence*** will make the world a more wonderful and musical place for Elliot and other children in the future.

Creative Sequence Online

http://cs.cedarrivermusic.com

Invitation Code: **CSO8B4MK0K**

Searchable Folk Song Database
Folk Song Scores with Playback
Curriculum Planning Templates
Lesson Plan Templates

Contents

About the Creative Sequence Series	1
The Importance of Creativity & Active Engagement	3
Designing a Creative Sequence	7
The Four Components of the Creative Sequence	9
Elements	11
Repertoire	33
Media	45
Process	53
Synthesizing, Organizing, and Writing Lesson Plans	61
Assessment	75
Creative Sequence and the NAfME National Standards	79
Creative Sequence and 21st Century Skills	81
Moving Forward with Creative Sequence and Your Classroom	83
Resources and References	85

About the *Creative Sequence* Series

Welcome to **Creative Sequence**! Creative Sequence is for the professional music educator who is looking to combine creative, student-centered activities and processes with organized, sequential objectives and assessments. Because every school, class, and student is unique, this book will *not* provide you with a rigid day-to-day set of lesson plans. Rather, it will guide you in developing a curriculum and writing lesson plans to fit *your* particular classroom needs. Everything in this volume is designed to make you think, question, explore, play, and create beautiful learning experiences with your classes.

Creative Sequence is designed to be a structural framework for your teaching, where you can both organize your existing materials and insert new ideas into your lessons. Future **CS** supplements will provide ready-made sequences and model lessons based on different musical elements, beginning with *Rhythm* and *Melody*. Each volume will be modular and fully customizable, to meet your needs.

In addition, by purchasing this volume, you get free access to the **Creative Sequence Online** web resources, at cs.cedarrivermusic.com, including a searchable database of folk songs and rhymes, curriculum and lesson plan templates, and a discussion forum for asking questions and sharing ideas!

Creative Sequence owes a great debt to the works of Carl Orff, Gunild Keetman, and the hundreds of dedicated music educators who have helped spread, shape, and grow Orff Schulwerk around the United States and the world. While **CS** is designed to be usable by music teachers with no background in Orff Schulwerk, it is recommended that you check out the American Orff Schulwerk Association (www.aosa.org) for more creative inspirations and training.

The Importance of Creativity and Active Engagement in the Music Classroom

Children today are bombarded with "media" and "entertainment." These passive and/or interactive technologies have, for over a century now, replaced many more traditional activities. Instead of playing ball, we watch a ballgame on TV, or use a controller to make a digital avatar "play" the sport in a video game. Instead of making music with our own voice or an acoustic instrument, we listen passively to a recording, or strum a plastic controller along with a prerecorded track.

While there are many ways in which the technological explosion of the past hundred years has enriched and expanded our lives, **Creative Sequence** is based on the premise that music, dance, drama, art, and physical activity are still essential human activities that *every child should learn to DO,* not just watch. Children inherently love to move, drum on things, make noise, and explore their environment. As teachers, it is our duty to engage this natural tendency, and to lead them to discover the joys of an active lifestyle.

The primary goal of quality music education is **guiding children to create, love, and learn about music**. Notice that, in this list, learning *about* music is the last item. The rationale is simple. Children who love and are engaged in a subject will want to learn more about that subject. Children who are not actively engaged will learn only when forced, and retain as little as possible when they leave your room.

All children *can* and *should* learn to make music.

To some, this statement may seem obvious. Yet, despite plenty

of evidence to the contrary, some still hold to the antiquated notion that singing and music-making are "talents" gifted to a few children at birth. This flies in the face of modern educational psychology, cultural evidence from around the world, and the day-to-day experience of parents and educators with young children.

Children learn at varying paces, according to their background, interest, and attention span. Of course, there are students who struggle with certain musical skills. Many students also struggle to learn mathematics or reading. No one questions the basic assumption that all students (excepting those with serious disabilities) will master these skills. When it comes to music and the arts, we should accept no less for our children.

In cultures around the world where technology has not yet completely changed the pace of everyday life, there are numerous examples of entire villages where music is a community activity in which everyone participates. Even in more advanced societies, there are pockets of close-knit communities where music and dance remain vital to social events. Unfortunately, mainstream Western culture supplants community gatherings altogether with digital communication, single-family homes, and private transportation. No wonder we seek to fill our desire for artistic expression by turning to the pre-recorded music of professionals.

If musical expression is going to remain an integral part of the human existence, it must start in the home, the preschool or elementary school. By the time most students are given the choice to play in an ensemble like band or orchestra, many have already made up their minds about whether they consider themselves musicians or not.

All other curricular objectives, *including music literacy*, are secondary to a positive, expressive experience making music.

Toddlers must speak before reading language. They must be able to count before identifying numerals. Yet as trained musicians, we educators have spent so much time learning and perfecting our reading skills that we often equate notation with music. In fact, the English language encourages this confusion by calling paper notation "sheet music" or even just "music." You hear trained musicians use this all the time. ("I forgot my music! Can you see the music?")

Let's be very clear. Music does *not* exist on paper. Music is human expression in sounds organized through time. *Notation* is the written record of what a piece of music should sound like. Therefore, music *literacy* should only be taught at the appropriate time, and following the appropriate development of musical *skills*.

Appreciation of music arises naturally from making music, and exploration of cultures, styles, and history should be interactive whenever possible.

The advantages of modern society and technology include affordable means to record, play back, and share music around the world, as well as access masterpieces from throughout history. What once required musicologists to travel the globe and attend universities with large research libraries can now be found online and for free. Music teachers must take advantage of these technologies, showing their children the songs, games, and styles of music from different corners of the globe. They should compile at least a cursory introduction to music history, highlighting famous pieces (Bach's *Prelude & Fugue*, Pachelbel's *Canon*, Beethoven's *5th Symphony*, Copland's *Appalachian Spring*, etc.)

The danger of teaching children music history and culture, however, is that it can be a passive experience. Children sit at desks silently for so much of the day, and have so little time in music class, that they should be actively involved whenever possible. Instead of simply listening and talking about musical examples, students can draw a picture while listening, or move expressively to the storyline. Choose musical excerpts from various styles that children can recreate and explore on barred percussion, recorder, or singing. When studying a time period or culture, look at not just the music, but the dances and games that accompany the music. By interacting and performing the arts of another culture, students can learn to embrace differences in all aspects of life.

Music should be a *creative* art, not simply a *recreative* art.

Our final guiding principle highlights the different ways of "making" music. When vocalists and instrumentalists in our Western culture traditionally perform a work, they are re-creating the music of a composer. All the basic musical elements - melody, rhythm, form, dynamics, tempo - are laid out in the score. Of course, great performers and ensembles make interpretations to go beyond the written notation. But the piece is essentially unchanged in any serious details.

This is not the only way to make music. Jazz musicians, folk musicians, and pop artists are much more accustomed to adapting, arranging, or even composing or improvising their own music. Composers create everything from lullabies to symphonies by writing new melodies, rhythms, and forms. By manipulating the very materials that make up a composition, these musicians gain a greater depth of understanding and sense of ownership in the resulting performance.

Children can and should be led to take this same ownership of their musical experiences. Rather than all of the decisions being made by the composer or the teacher/director, the master teacher guides his or her students to make creative choices. Students can compose accompaniments based on repeated ostinato patterns, improvise solos on given scales and phrase patterns, choreograph dances and games to accompany a song, and combine all of this to create longer performances out of simple songs.

Designing a _Creative Sequence_

Many books, courses, school districts, states, and other organizations have spent considerable time detailing the proper expectations and sequences for teaching music in schools. Some are called Standards and Benchmarks, Grade Level Expectations, Curriculum Objectives, or simply Goals. The solid theory behind all of these curricula is that students must learn music in a particular order, beginning with basic, simple concepts like keeping a steady beat and matching pitch, and progressing to more advanced concepts, like sight-reading a song in D minor.

Most music textbook publishers create their own curricula with every objective listed in precise order, accompanied by a complete lesson, often made so "user friendly" (singalong CD, step-by-step directions, copyable worksheets) as to nearly eliminate the need for a music specialist at all!

The problem with all such curricula is that they were not written by you, for your students, your schedule, or your school. While they provide an excellent starting point for the beginning teacher, it does not take long to realize that adaptability and creativity are not only desired in teaching music, but essential to meeting the needs of your students. A particular class might not be ready for a particular lesson, or an upcoming concert means putting the curriculum "on hold" until after the performance. Textbooks can also can be constraining, as a new lesson or song picked up at a workshop needs to be "fit" into the existing curriculum. By the end of the year, it is very likely that a whole year's goals have not been accomplished. Depending on how the book is laid out and followed, this can lead to missing the same parts of the curriculum at the end of every year.

More importantly, following a textbook means missing out on opportunities to create cross-curricular connections with reading, math, science, social studies, art, physical education, or any other subject.

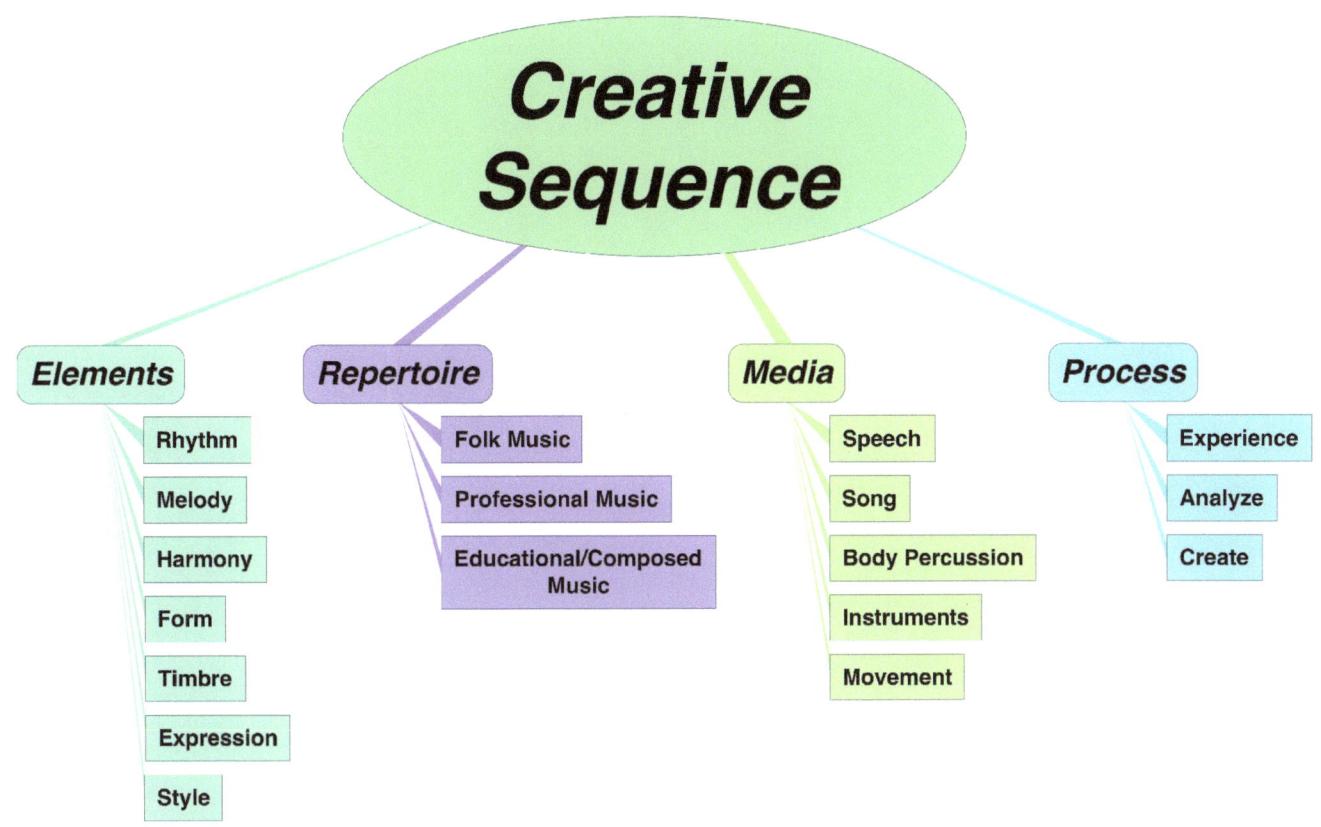

The Four Components of the Creative Sequence
Elements, Repertoire, Media & Process

Creative Sequence begins with an awareness of different types of skills and knowledge. *Elements*, such as rhythm and melody, make up pieces of music, known as the *Repertoire*. This repertoire is created, learned, performed, and analyzed through a *Process*, using various *Media*, including singing and playing instruments. By focusing on these four, easy to remember components, *CS* provides a clear template for facilitating exceptional learning.

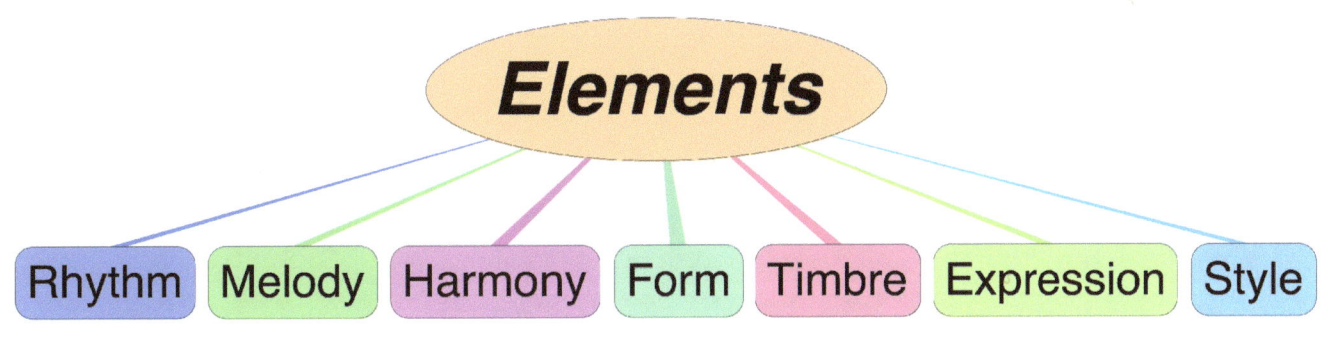

Elements

The Elements are the fundamental building-blocks of music. Any piece can be broken down and analyzed, or newly composed, from these blocks. What follows is a description of each Element, and a partial list of sub-Elements and individual musical concepts to be taught. The lists are not meant to be exhaustive, but rather to be the springboard for your own creative sequencing. After reading through this section, consider writing out your own list of concepts.

CS is designed to be taught as a spiral curriculum. For instance, steady beat is listed as one of the first rhythmic goals, but this skill is revisited and strengthened throughout the years. Many detailed curricula will be written by grade, or even by month or week. The goal of *CS* is to show the flow of each element, from simple to complex. You may wish to delineate what goals each grade is expected to achieve. Yet keep in mind that our best guess in the fall is likely going to be a bit off by the spring. By maintaining a continuous list of concepts, we can start our second year by simply picking up where we left off (with review, of course). When following a pre-printed curriculum, the danger is to simply skip what isn't covered at the end of the year.

Priorities and balance are two things to consider when writing and teaching elemental concepts. What is more important, singing on pitch or identifying letter names? What takes more time to teach, compound meter or dynamics? Begin with clear priorities, and make sure your students can achieve these first.

Finally, remember that each element does not exist in isolation. Four elements should always exist: Rhythm, Form, Style, & Expression. Melody and Harmony are not necessarily there on every activity (drumming a single part, for example), but are still present much of the time. Each lesson, then, can actually cover multiple elements at the same time!

Rhythm

Beat/Pulse
- steady beat
- fast vs. slow
- tempo
- quarter note
- offbeat
- syncopation

Divisions
- word rhythms
- simple divisions
- eighth notes
- sixteenth notes
- eighth/sixteenth combinations
- compound divisions

Long Durations
- sustained sounds
- tie
- half notes
- whole notes
- dotted half notes
- dotted quarter notes

Rests
- sound vs. silence
- silent beat
- quarter rest
- half rest
- whole rest
- dotted half rest
- eighth rest

Meters
- simple 2
- simple 3
- simple 4
- 2/4 time signature
- 3/4 time signature
- 4/4 time signature
- compound 2
- 6/8 time signature
- simple 5
- 5/4 time signature

Rhythm

Rhythm is the single-most important element in music. Without organization of time, there is no music. The study of beat and rhythm is tied to the pulse of our hearts, the sway of our steps, and the patter of our language. Any child who can walk steadily and speak fluently can learn to keep a beat and perform a rhythm.

CS suggests learning rhythmic patterns by beginning with familiar speech patterns, such as students' names, chanted to a beat. Identify the number of syllables in each name, and play around with the pattern by reorganizing students. When notation is introduced, you can still use speech to read and compose rhythms (examples: grape, carrot, celery, watermelon; Mars, Venus, Jupiter, Solar System) while reinforcing the theme of a song or a unit from another class. Some teachers find a rhythmic syllable system (i.e.: ta, titi, tiritiri) helps maintain consistency for their class. While these can certainly produce excellent reading results, be careful that students understand the difference between a *name* and a *syllable*.

Notation of rhythms is quite a bit more complex than performing rhythms. Do not confuse reading difficulties with performance difficulties! Make sure your students can *do* the skill before *reading* the skill. While 6/8 time may be challenging to teach and read, every Kindergarten class learns to speak or sing *Hickory Dickory Dock*, in perfect 6/8 time!

Rhythmic concepts move clearly from simple to complex, and can form the backbone of your sequence.

Melody

Matching Pitch
- high vs. low
- exploring the voice
- upper register (head voice)
- lower register (chest voice)
- transposition

Notation
- staff
- treble clef
- lines & spaces
- letter names
- bass clef
- grand staff

Tones & Scales
- so-mi
- la-so-mi
- so-mi-do
- mi-re-do
- Tonic
- do Pentatonic on F
- do Pentatonic on C
- do Pentatonic on G
- la Pentatonic on D
- la Pentatonic on A
- la Pentatonic on E
- re Pentatonic on D
- so Pentatonic on D
- do Hexatonic
- la Hexatonic
- Ionian (Major - do)
- Aeolian (Minor - la)
- Dorian (re)
- Phrygian (mi)
- Lydian (fa)
- Mixolydian (so)
- Blues Scales

Melody

The second most important musical element is melody. It is essential to singing and performing on pitched instruments. A clear sequence begins with helping students explore their voice, match pitch in various ranges, and then begin to build a vocabulary of intervals for performance, creativity, and reading. From two-note and three-note songs, the range and repertoire expands to eventually explore many diatonic modes and specialized scales, such as blues scales.

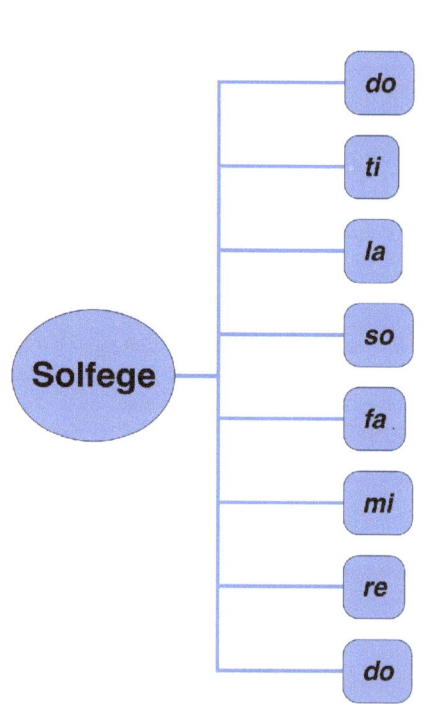

While letter names are important for instrumental reading, for singing and some mallet percussion work **CS** recommends using the moveable-*do* solfege system, in which the intervals between syllables always remain constant. For major keys and gapped scales (such as *do* Pentatonic) that have a major third above the tonic, the tonic is always labeled *do*. Other scales can then be identified as variants, by changing the tonic note. Pentatonic scales can be centered on *do*, *re*, *mi*, *so*, or *la*, and are labeled by their tonic syllable and pitch name (i.e., *la* Pentatonic on E). Diatonic scales can be labeled by the Medieval modes: Ionian (*do*), Dorian (*re*), Phrygian (*mi*), Lydian (*fa*), Mixolydian (*so*), and Aeolian (*la*). All of these scales are common in world folk music, with the exceptions of *mi* Pentatonic and Lydian.

Expressive speech and vocal exploration are the foundation of singing. While many students will learn to match pitch easily (or have already mastered this skill at home), others will require serious exploration and encouragement to find their upper register. If a student cannot match pitch easily, he often speaks with little expression or varied pitch.

Student naturally speak, and sometimes sing, in their lower register (chest voice). In order to help students find their upper register (head voice), begin two-note *so-mi* songs and chants on C-A (F=*do*). This range is high enough to distinguish from the lower register (chest voice), while still easily within children's reach.

Instruments such as xylophones and recorders provide students with a concrete, kinesthetic and visual way of experiencing melody. The precise pitches and sequential layout of barred instruments allow students to understand and explore intervals and melodic patterns with very little technical skill. It also gives the child who struggles with singing on pitch a chance to master these concepts.

Staff notation is another important visual tool for students to identify, learn to use, and discover how to manipulate. While the basic symbols can be used in conjunction with the solfege system mentioned above, the use of absolute letter names should be taught when the class is ready to use these letter names on a barred instrument. The visual labels on each bar allow students to quickly grasp the rationale behind letter names, and gives purpose to the memorization of silly phrases such as *"Every Good Boy Does Fine."*

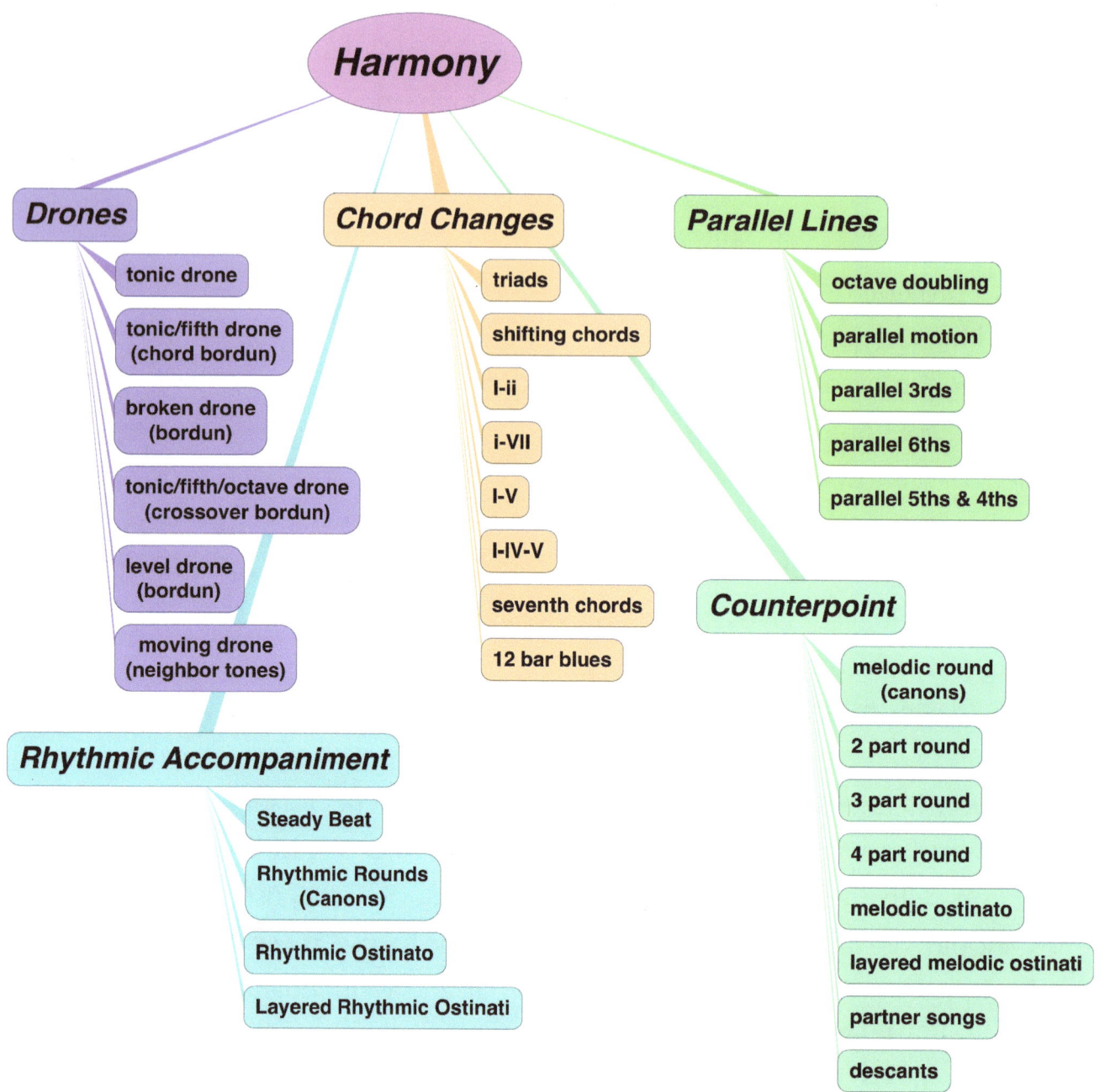

Harmony

Harmony as learned by music majors in college is an advanced subject, with chord progressions, counterpoint, and voice leading. Yet many folk traditions begin with nothing so complex. Rather, the drone, one sustained tone or an open fifth, becomes the root of an open, non-progressing harmonization. This is then extended with short repeated patterns, or ostinati, both rhythmic and melodic. Rounds and partner songs introduce true independent parts, and only then are parallel harmonies, counterpoint, and functional chords introduced.

Drones and ostinati are important for children because they make harmony accessible and performable. By using one or two bars on a xylophone and a simple rhythm pattern, for example, young students can easily accompany a song. Ostinato patterns also provide an opportunity for students to manipulate rhythmic and melodic elements to create their own patterns.

Rhythmic accompaniment, while not technically "harmonic," is included here because of its function. Like harmony, layered rhythms add complexity and depth to simple songs.

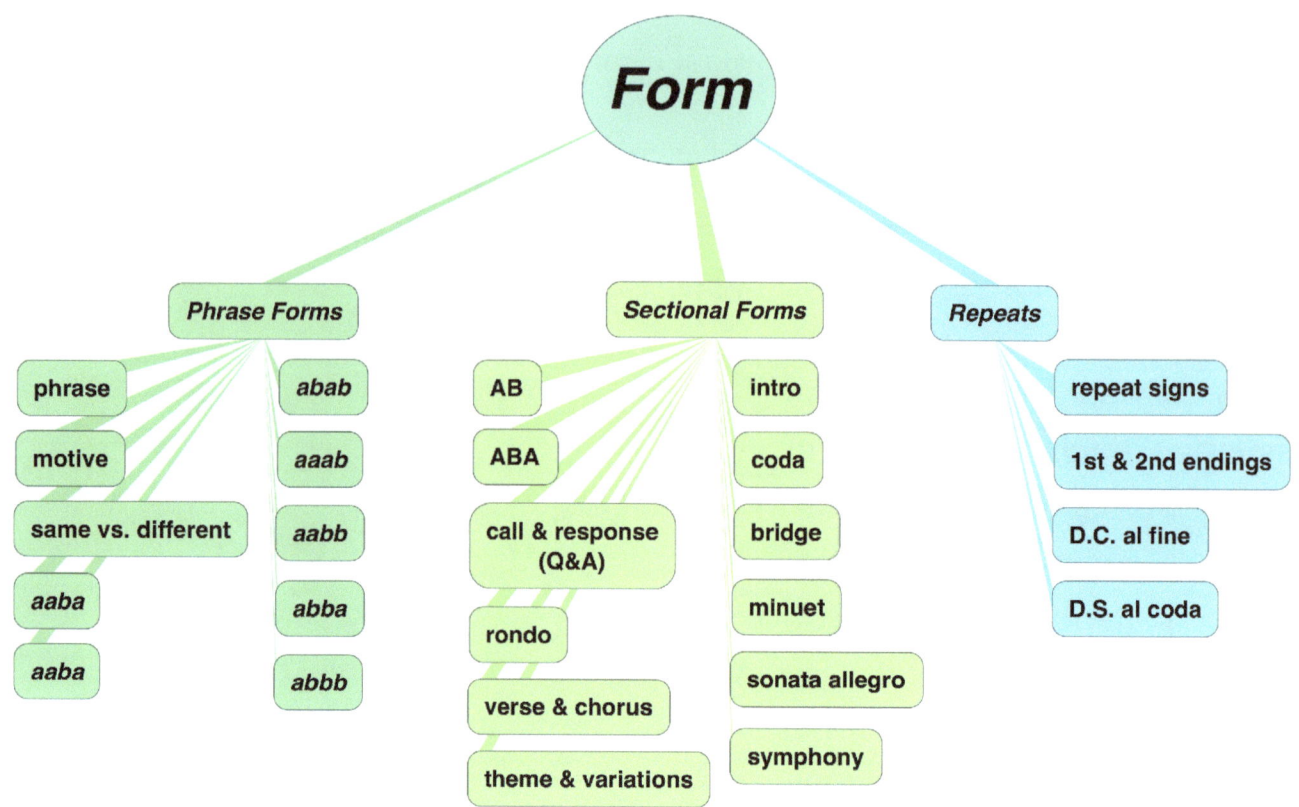

Form

Like harmony, form begins very simply, as an understanding of repetition and change. Phrase forms, which are common in nursery rhymes and simple songs, are identified and used for creative work in the early stages. Later, large forms like rondo, theme & variations, and sonata allegro can be introduced.

> *Go to bed, Tom!*
> *Go to bed, Tom!*
> *Tired or not, Tired or not,*
> *Go to bed, Tom!*

Phrase forms allow students to identify the structure of poetry and music. (The pattern 'aaba' is probably the most common in children's rhymes). They can then use these simple patterns as the basis for exploration, improvisation, or composition with new text, rhythmic, or melodic ideas.

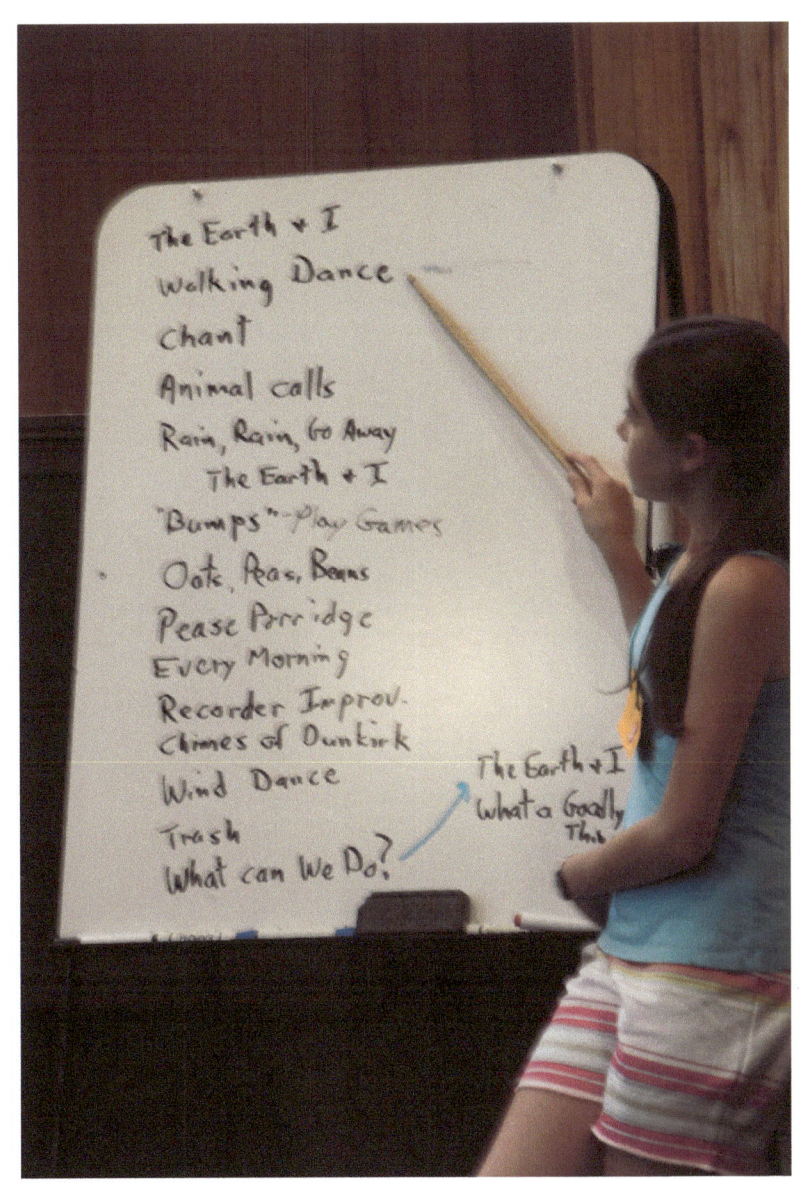

Simple sectional forms can provide a performance structure, within which children can compose, improvise, or arrange individual sections. Call & Response allows an improvised phrase to be followed by a standard response. Question & Answer form allows students to improvise an answer based on a partner's question. Rondo (ABACADA...) allows many individuals or small groups to perform, with an A section theme to tie together all the parts.

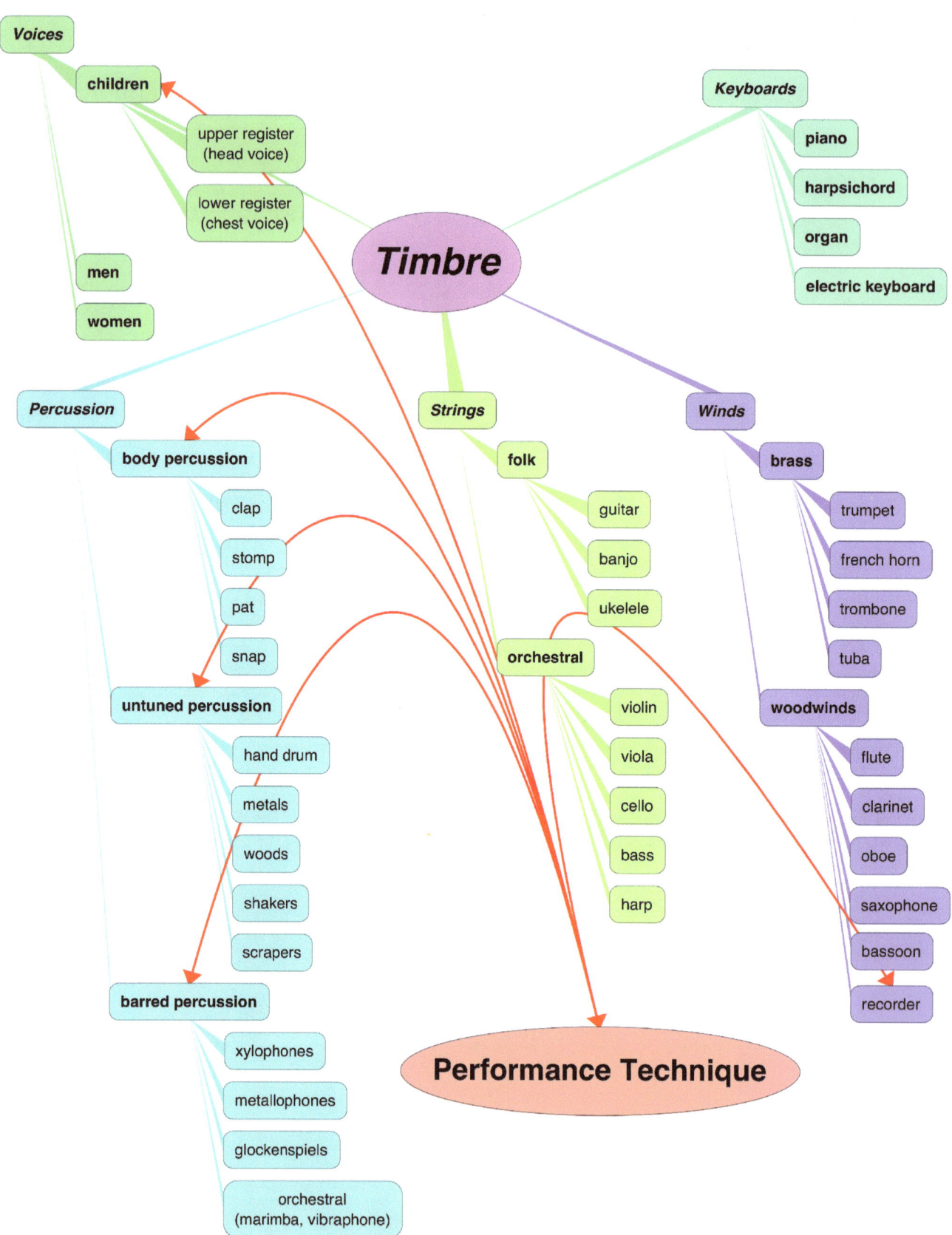

Timbre

Timbre is the quality of sounds. Scientifically, it is the shape of the soundwave, including a fundamental pitch and various overtones, that makes each instrument and voice sound unique. Timbre is probably the simplest element to combine with other goals. Rather than it being a focus of lesson-writing, it can be taught organically, as different instruments and voice qualities are explored throughout the curriculum.

When studying instruments and singing, it is of course necessary to also focus on *Performance Technique*. Teachers should be familiar with supported, unstrained singing techniques for children, basic mallet techniques for barred percussion, hand drum technique, and recorder breath, fingering, and tonguing.

The particular elementary ensemble outlined in the *Media* chapter includes barred percussion (i.e., xylophone, glockenspiel), unpitched percussion (hand drums, wood blocks), and the recorder. There are several reasons to utilize this traditional ensemble. First, unlike other keyboard instruments (piano, electric keyboard), barred percussion are designed to be used in a large ensemble (everyone can play together at once) and utilize gross motor skills, rather than fine motor finger motions. This allows success at a younger age, and in large class groups. Percussion, especially hand drums, can likewise be taught to large groups at a time, and do not require a complicated technique to make a decent sound.

The recorder, on the other hand, is a more advanced instrument. Usually not introduced before 3rd grade, the recorder allows students to experience sustained wind sounds, at a cost that makes it possible to once again provide instruments to the entire class. Despite their low cost, however, the recorder is a professional instrument. Teachers should take care to learn proper technique, and be able to demonstrate quality tone.

For other instruments not available in large quantities to your children, it is always ideal to have a live demonstration, with quick turns trying it out if possible. A field trip to a regional orchestra, or inviting the high school band to come to your school, can help make this interesting. When not feasible, a video or quality audio recording and pictures can serve to introduce various instruments. Remember to keep the children involved, either through discussion, reflective writing, drawing, or moving to the music.

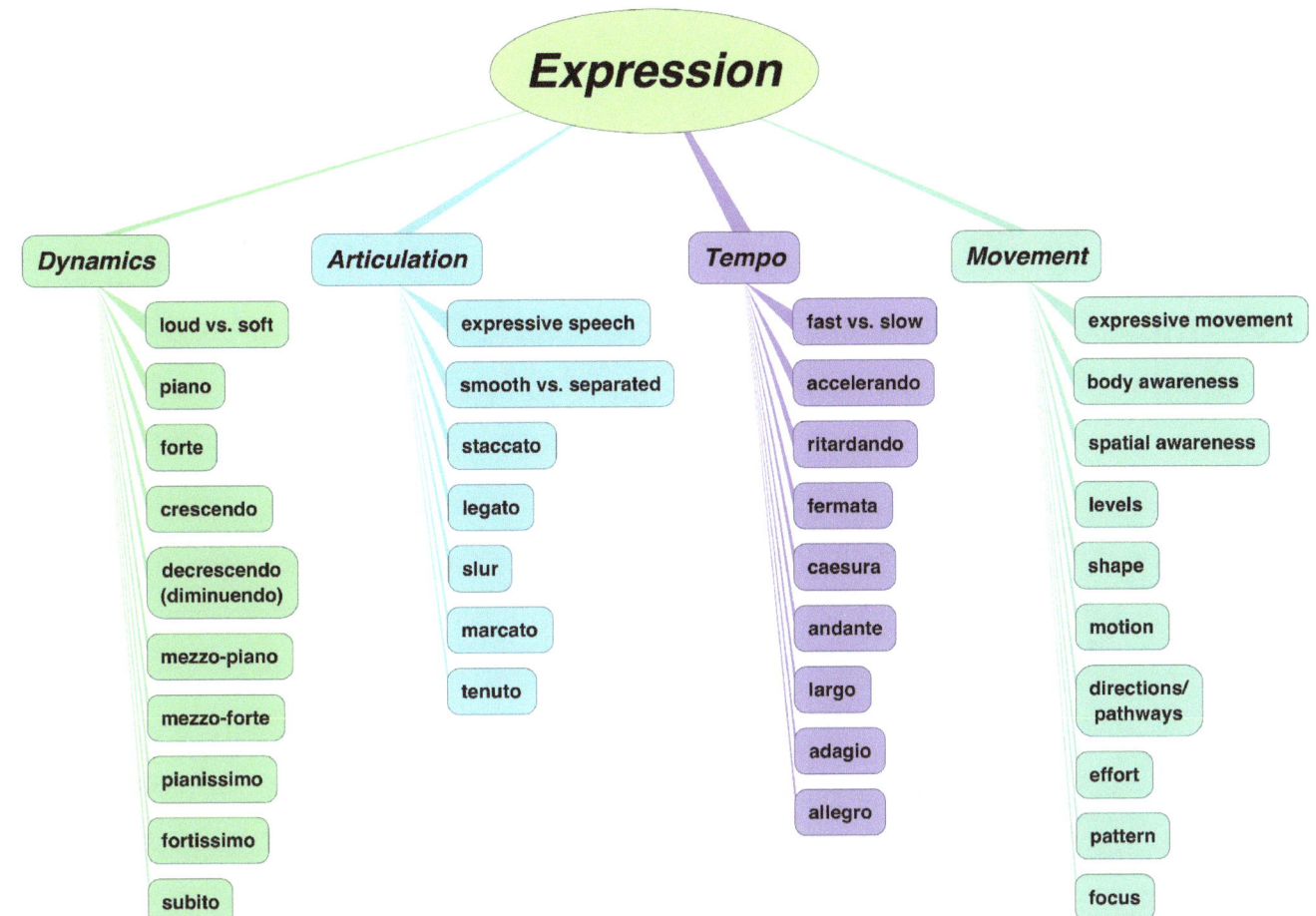

Expression

The term expression combines four different smaller performance elements: *Dynamics, Articulations, Tempo,* and *Movement.*

Dynamics can be easily tied into any existing lesson, but work particularly well in expressive storytelling activities, or with songs which evoke stories. While simple dynamic contrasts (loud vs. soft, *forte* vs. *piano*) are very easy for students to pick up in a short amount of time, it does take practice for students to achieve various mid-level dynamics. *Decrescendo* is particularly notorious for being difficult, as the natural instinct is to get suddenly soft.

Articulations allow performers to create a variety of different effects in a musical line. This is particularly easy to apply to the recorder and other wind performances, but can also be used to good effect in choral singing.

Tempo represents the speed of the underlying beat in the music. Since beat exploration and performance are started at the very beginning of musical study, tempo exploration should begin early on as well. Labeling terms can wait until later. Students do enjoy learning the Italian words, however!

Movement is truly its own art form, and placing it under the Expression element does not do it justice. Yet it is so important to connect to our musical experiences, and creative dance is truly all about "expression." By exploring the physical space around them, students become attuned to their own bodies, connected to the music, and freed to express themselves without hesitation. Just as for singing, it is up to the music teacher to create an atmosphere of complete acceptance, where students can and will leave their comfort zones. We will discuss the importance of movement more in the *Media* chapter.

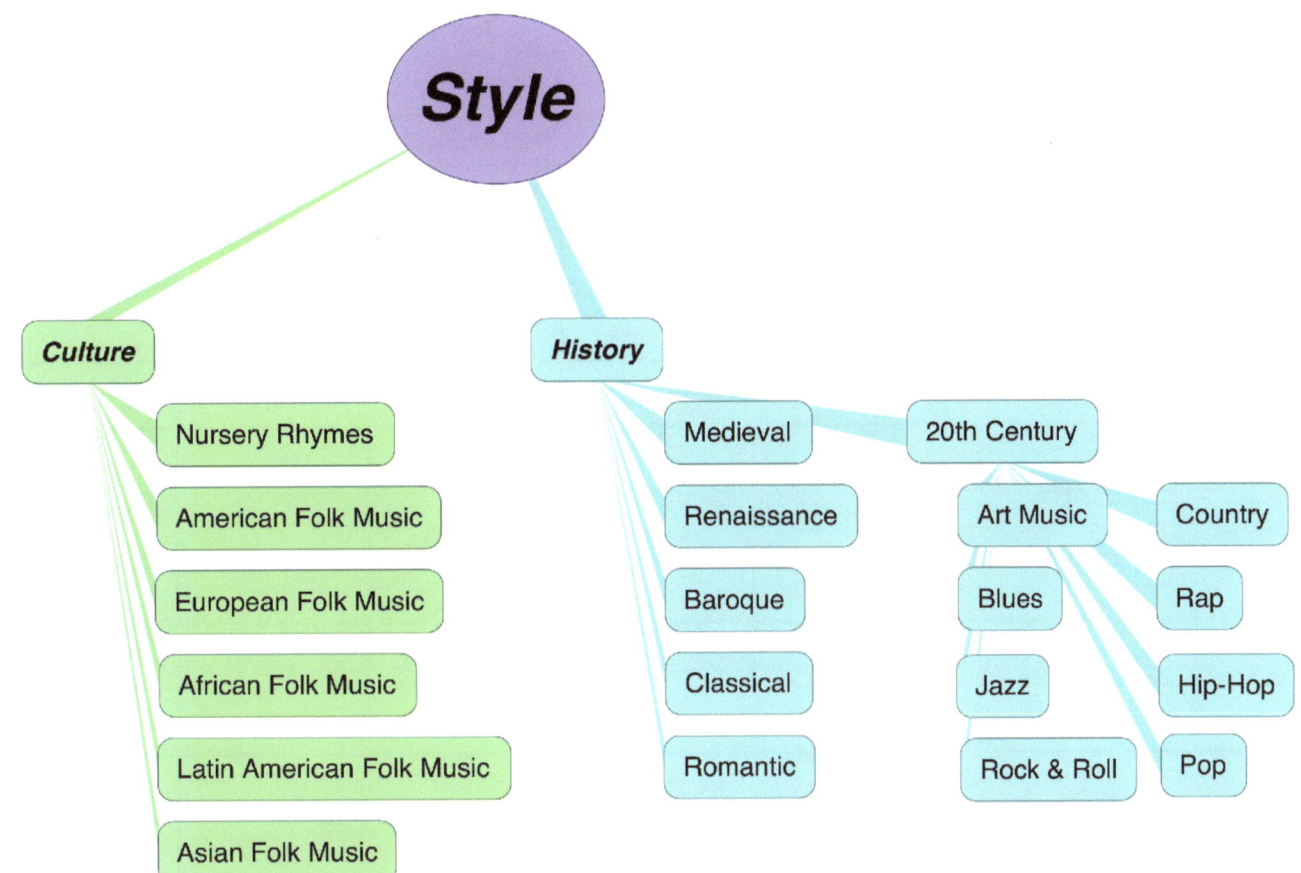

Style

Style refers to the culture, historical period, and genre of a particular piece of music. A thorough curriculum will study music of folk cultures around the world, historical time periods of musical development, and modern genres of music. The wonderful and terrifying aspect of style is that it is too broad to ever be completely learned. Therefore, priorities must be established, in choosing music that students can interact with, perform, and learn about their world. The chapter on *Repertoire* will deal more with this subject. Style is included here as an element to make it part of your checklist of concepts.

Creative Sequence
Elemental Music Map of Concepts

Rhythm	Melody	Harmony	Form	Timbre	Expression	Style

Mapping the Elements

In order to teach all these elements, we must decide what to teach when. Some sequences seem obvious (steady beat competency comes before sixteenth notes, pentatonic scales before diatonic), while others are more arbitrary (studying European music before Asian music). Here are some rules to follow when writing your own music element map.

1. The order and sequence is up to you.

Many concepts are listed in a rather arbitrary fashion. This is true in every published list of this kind. No publisher can foresee your schedule, your students, or your training. They don't know that your First Grade class learned about the orchestra on a field trip, or that your Fifth Grade class has not yet really tackled sixteenth notes (don't ask why, you don't want to know). What fits into one school's year may take two years at another school. You must look at where your students are *now* before you decide where they should go next.

2. You can't teach everything (at least not right away).

Set the sequence so that your priorities are met. Decide on 3-4 "essential" goals for each class to achieve, and make sure they succeed. During the first year, you will be rewriting your goals a lot. This is normal and healthy.

3. Keep high expectations.

Despite the limitations of your time, resources, and support, expect great results from yourself and your students. When expectations are low, students and teachers achieve them and then feel satisfied. Yet when expectations are raised, they are often still met, to the surprise of all involved! Don't sell yourself or your students short on what is possible.

4. Think about connections between Elements.

Why would the March style be taught in Year 1, and Waltz taught in Year 3? Because Year 1 students are learning to march to a beat, and Year 3 students are identifying and notating in 3/4 time. Whenever possible, identify places that a single song or game can achieve multiple goals at once.

5. Each concept is actually many stages.

In the chapter on *Process* we will discuss the many stages that need to occur for students to learn a concept. This process may stretch over weeks, months, or even years. Students may learn to perform sixteenth notes in 2nd or 3rd grade, but not read and compose using them until 4th grade.

6. Be flexible!

Regardless of what you write on this chart, do not hesitate to teach a new concept as it arises organically in your classroom. Students are often the best judges of what they are ready to learn.

	Creative Sequence Lesson Plan with *Elemental Objectives*
Grade/Class	Kindergarten/First Grade
Date	September 2012
Primary Elemental Objective	**Rhythm:** Maintain a steady beat to accompany a song.
Secondary Elemental Objectives	**Timbre**: Explore classroom unpitched percussion instruments. **Rhythm**: Sing a rhythmic text.
National/State Standard	NSME #2, 6 P21 - Collaboration, Leadership, Innovation, Accountability
Repertoire	*The Ants Go Marching One By One*
Media	Singing Clapping Unpitched Percussion Movement
Process - *Explore* - *Analyze* - *Create*	1. While class sits on the floor, the teacher introduces the song by singing (accompany self with guitar/autoharp/etc.) Ask the class to pat the beat on their knees as you sing. 2. Ask each student to choose a different way of keeping the beat (clapping, patting shoulders, etc.) The whole class should copy each student for one verse. 3. Have the class get up and march to the beat, following each other in a line around the room, while you continue to sing. 4. Replace the words "the last one" with a student's name, and ask that student to go choose an untuned percussion instrument to play while marching. 5. On each verse, choose a new student and add an instrument. You can select instruments that match the idea of each verse, or let students decide. You will probably have to go through the song 2-3 times to give everyone a turn. WARNING: this gets LOUD. Have a cue to get attention ready before you begin. 6. Return the class to the floor, and have them take turns or play together (depending on your instruments) on the steady beat. Talk about each kind of unpitched instrument, its name, and how it works. 7. Take out the instruments and ask the class to sing the song with you.
Assessments	Take time to quickly document students who appear to not be able to find the beat, and give them one-on-one assistance during the lesson or in the near future.

The Ants Go Marching

Traditional Children's Lyrics   Irish Tune

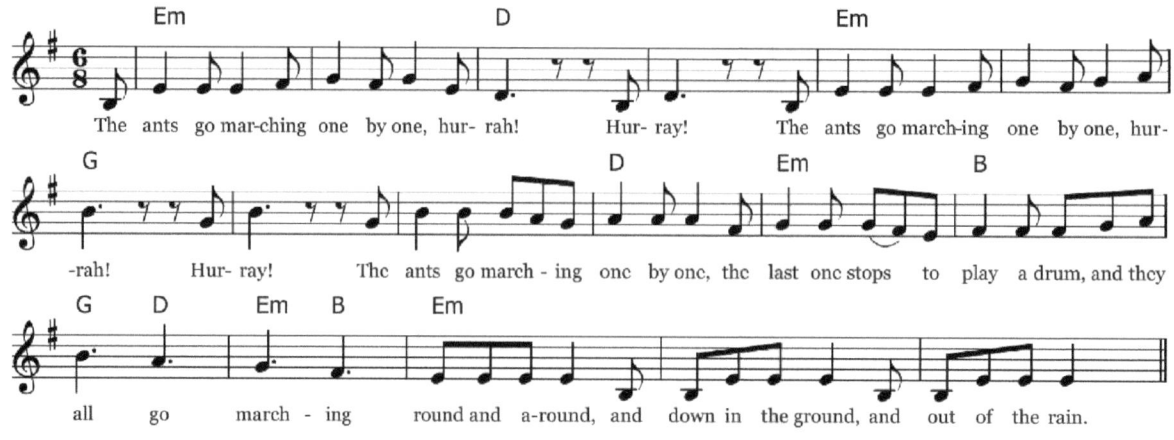

2x2 - tie his shoe
3x3 - climb a tree
4x4 - shut the door
5x5 - take a dive
6x6 - pick up sticks

7x7 - look up to heav'n
8x8 - close the gate
9x9 - pick up a dime
10x10 - sing it again! (OR) say, "The End!"

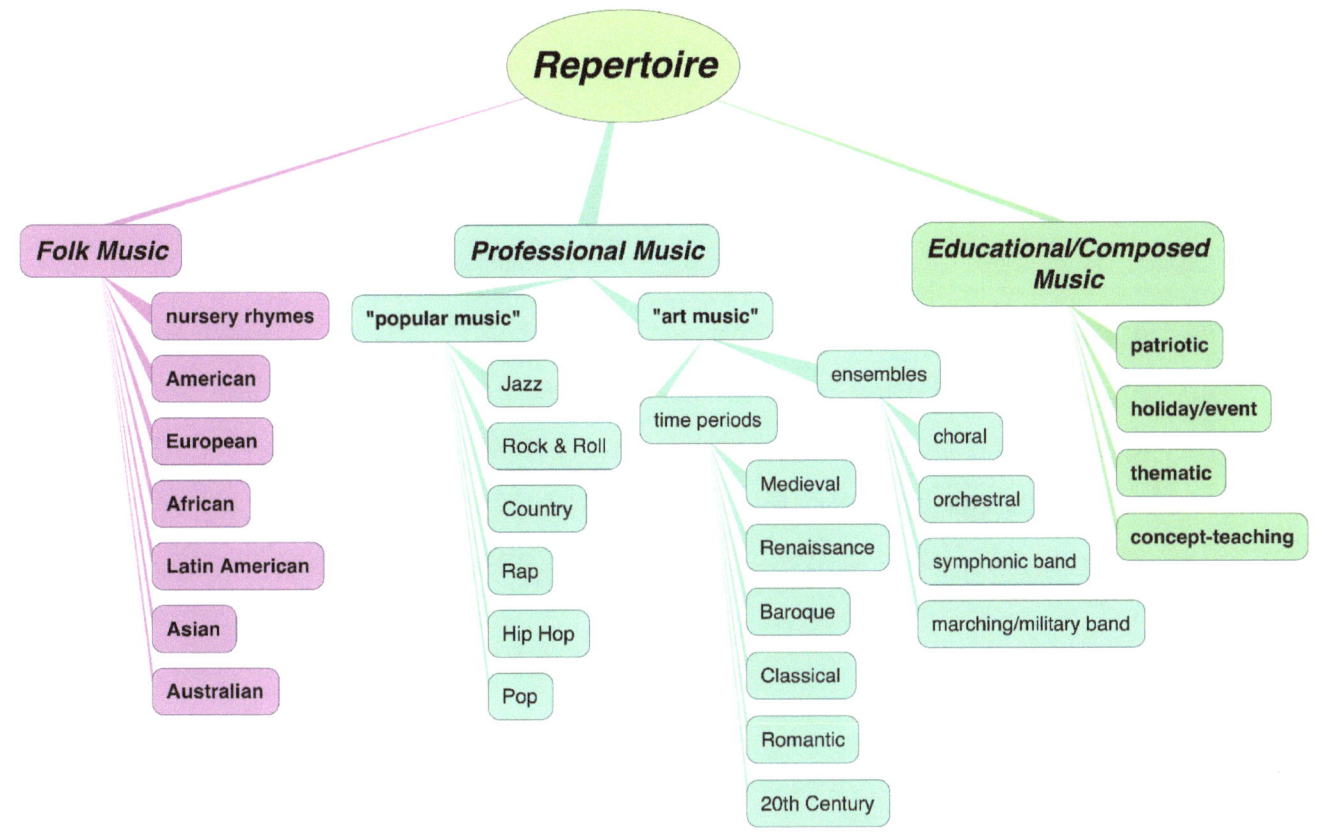

Repertoire

Repertoire is by far the largest and most non-standardized piece of the music curriculum. Choosing quality music can be incredibly time-consuming for the beginning teacher. Yet this step is crucial to creating your own cohesive curriculum.

Some educators believe that there should be a "standard" repertoire that every child should learn, so that we might grow together as a society. While there are certainly some songs that fit this "universal" ideal in the US (*Happy Birthday*, *Twinkle Twinkle*, *Jingle Bells*, etc.), they are so common that the music teacher does not even need to teach them. The problem with developing a larger standardized repertoire is that no one will ever agree on everything to be included or excluded. There is simply too much quality music in the world today to teach it all to our children.

Instead, we must prioritize what our students will learn, based on their musical and cultural needs. Elementary music repertoire can set the stage for lifelong music making and open children's minds to people and cultures from around the globe.

Folk Music

Folk music means, simply enough, "music of the folk." It is the music that is most familiar to a culture because it is sung by parents to children, or as an entire community together. Unfortunately, much of the folk music culture in the US has been lost along with our sense of community, and has been replaced with digital, passive entertainment. Yet at the same time, our modern technology has allowed unprecedented access to our own cultural roots *and* that of people from around the world.

Folk music provides easy, accessible songs, dances, and games that children can learn to perform by themselves. It is written to be performed by *everyone*, not just trained professionals. It also gives a deep historical perspective, connecting children to that time when everyone *made* music for entertainment, and hopefully bringing back a little of that into their lives.

American Folk Music

American folk music is, like our nation itself, a mix of many different cultures coming together, influencing each other, and becoming something new. Music of European settlers sounded much like the music in their home countries. Slaves brought from Africa, while being mixed and forced to speak English, maintained stylistic components from their ancestors' music (complex rhythms, sliding pitches, call & response forms) that set African-American music apart. Immigrants from Latin America have now also transformed our folk culture, with an influx of Spanish language, and the heritage of many different nations.

Labeling American folk music then becomes a challenge. If we label music as "African American" or "Latino American," then the term "European American" should be considered for completeness and fairness. These labels are only useful as far as they help students identify the cultural roots of songs, and make connections to the music of other countries and continents. Later folk styles, like Blues, connect various traditions together, while also leading the way towards modern popular music styles.

American folk music can also include patriotic standards, like *America the Beautiful, My Country 'Tis of Thee*, and *The Star-Spangled Banner.*

World Folk Music

World folk music provides music teachers an opportunity to prepare students for the interconnected, global society in which they will live. By learning a bit of foreign language, playing a game, and singing a song, students can learn to appreciate both the *similarities* and *differences* between other parts of the world and their own society.

Folk Dance, Folk Poetry (Nursery Rhymes), & Children's Games

Music is not the only art form that is shared in community settings. Folk dances and children's games from around the world can be learned jointly with the music that accompanies them. Poetry, especially Nursery Rhymes, can provide young children with the rhythmic fluency they need to be effective speakers *and* musicians.

Folk Music vs. Composed Music

There is some overlap between the definitions of *folk music*, which is music handed down through an oral process, and *composed* music, which has a clear author, and is usually notated. *Jingle Bells* was composed in 1850 by James Lord Pierpont. Yet most of us know it by singing along at holiday gatherings, or learned it in elementary school. It has become a folk song, but we should still, whenever possible, give credit to Mr. Pierpont and other composers for their work.

Educational/Composed Music

Folk music can cover many elements of music while exposing students to history and culture, but it also becomes necessary on occasion to supplement this with music composed in a particular scale, with a particular rhythm, or in a particular form. A great example of this type of music is *Music for Children* (Vols. 1-5, ed. Margaret Murray) by Carl Orff and Gunild Keetman. Within these volumes one can find, for example, a song in 3/4 time with a simple melody that introduces the scale tone *fa*. Since this music was written as examples for children, it is not required that it be learned or performed as written. Instead, each piece is a model that can be played with and rearranged. The teacher might only choose one section, one harmonic part, etc.; whatever suits the purpose of the lesson.

Other examples include music composed for particular holidays, groups, or special events. A school song would fall into this category, as would newer patriotic compositions, or a spooky fun Hallowe'en piece from a textbook series.

Whether starting with a folk song or a composed work, remember that the process goal with many lessons should be to have the children doing some of the creative work. The original piece should serve as a model that, when performed and analyzed, can be the springboard to student improvisation or composition.

Professional Music

This category of music includes "art" music from various time periods (Rennaisance, Baroque, Classical, etc.), and "popular" styles, like Jazz, Country, Rock & Roll, and Rap. The term Professional Music points out that this music is primarily performed by professionals or trained hobbyists. It is not music that is designed to be performed by an entire community, with children, parents, and grandparents.

Rather, there is a clear delineation between the audience (listeners or dancers) and the performers (vocalists and instrumentalists). While nearly all these styles have their roots in the American cross-pollination of African and European folk traditions, they have for the most part left the realm of community, interactive music, to become performance art for a passive audience.

The beauty of Professional Music lies in the ability of the composers and performers to achieve virtuosic solos, complex arrangements, and lengthy musical works that would not be possible with an untrained ensemble. It can serve as the model for cooperative learning, advanced music literacy, and professional applications of music. The challenge lies in the exclusive nature of the music. While children can dance to Professional Music, draw a picture in response to it, or have a discussion analyzing its features, this is not the same as singing, playing instruments, and creating the music oneself.

Remember our goal from the beginning, *guiding children to create, love, and learn about music*. Keep this in mind as you choose how to include Professional Music in your curriculum. Ask yourself if it is teaching them something valuable. Is the lesson interactive, or are they sitting still and unable to respond aesthetically? Has a recording or adult performance supplanted the possibility of the children making their own music? Is it acceptable to put on concerts where the children scream along with a pre-recorded soundtrack? This gives students a false understanding of what it means to make music. Confidence and skill can more fully develop when the children are responsible for their own arrangements, and are singing over simple, acoustic accompaniments.

Collecting Repertoire

Whenever you find a new resource, be it a book, workshop handout, or online source, it is helpful to catalogue each song, game, or dance according to its potential uses in your class. A simple spreadsheet like the one below can help you keep track of each piece. Then, you can have a digital file full of scanned or computer-notated scores to refer to when you need a particular piece. For access to the online, interactive ***Creative Sequence*** Repertoire Database, visit cs.cedarrivermusic.com/repertoire.

Creative Sequence Repertoire Collection Sample									
Music/ Dance/ Game	Origin/ Composer/ Style	Scale	Melodic Focus	Harmony	Time Signature	Rhythmic Focus #1	Rhythmic Focus #2	Form	Movement
Charlie Over the Ocean	American Children's Game	*do* Pentatonic	solo singing matching pitch	a cappella drone	6/8			Call & Resp. abab	Seated circle. Leader walks around circle while singing, class echos. On last word, leader taps another student, and that student chases the leader around the circle, a la *Duck Duck Goose*
Diddle Diddle Dumpling	Mother Goose Nursery Rhyme	speech			4/4	four sixteenth notes	eighth/two sixteenths	aa'ba	
Hotaru Koi	Japanese Folk Song	*la,-do,-re-mi* (*re* Pent., missing *so*)	*re* = tonic	drone, 2 part round	2/4	rest		abba	
Lost My Gold Ring	Jamaican Children's Game	*do* Pentatonic on F	accented *re*	I-V	2/2	syncopation	cut time	abab'	Circle formation; gold ring is hidden in one player's hands, all hold hands out, another student must guess who has it.
Yonder Mountain	Virginia Folk Song	*do* Pentatonic on G	low *la* low *so*	drone/ I-ii/ I-vi	3/4	anacrusis		aa'ba'	

Creative Sequence Repertoire Collection

Music/ Dance/ Game	Origin/ Composer/ Style	Scale	Melodic Focus	Harmony	Time Signature	Rhythmic Focus #1	Rhythmic Focus #2	Form	Movement

Choosing Repertoire

When selecting repertoire to use, teachers should first identify what their priority objectives and concepts are for that day, week, or unit. These include all of the *Elements*, as well as any cross-curricular concepts and upcoming special events.

Elements

Whenever possible, choose a song that will teach or review multiple concepts at the same time. For example, if you have many songs that are in *do* Pentatonic, then choose one that also fits the rhythmic concepts your children are working on. Or choose a Pentatonic song from a particular nationality or style that you want to introduce to the class. Arrange the song so that it includes harmony, dynamics, and a movement game that also align with your goals. It is not necessary to align *every* Element in every song, but the more connections you can make, the more time you save, and the more your students see the big picture.

Concerts, Holidays, & Assemblies

Any time your students need to perform in front of an audience, the preparation must be carefully integrated into your class, for at least 4-6 periods ahead of time. This does *NOT* mean switching into full production mode, where everything they have been working on is tossed out and replaced with a slick, pre-packaged show. Rather than "Performance," think "*Informance*"- a chance to demonstrate all of the wonderful things your students are learning and practicing in music class.

By choosing appropriate repertoire, you can create classroom activities where the students are still engaged in the creative process, right up until performance time. Allow students to apply their knowledge of the Elements to arrange the form of a piece, write an accompaniment part, or create a dance. Choose a picture book or other story to tie together multiple songs and games into a complete performance.

Make your selections of repertoire for performances as early as possible, to allow for the music to be integrated seamlessly into your lessons.

Cross-Curricular Connections

One popular theme in current educational philosophy is teaching connections across the curriculum, rather than teaching classes as independent, unrelated subjects. As a music specialist, take it upon yourself to seek out the classroom teachers, art specialist, and others to discuss how you might integrate your lessons together. Large unit themes in science, social studies, math, or literacy, are great starting points for exploratory music. Once you have collected this information, search out (or compose) music, poetry, stories, and other materials that you can use to connect to this theme. Important vocabulary words can also be used to make rhythmic word chains, even without an underlying song. If time allows, let the *students* create the music to illustrate their unit!

Another helpful way to reach out to classroom teachers is then to offer them recordings or documents of the resources that you have found, so that they may incorporate this into their lessons.

Be Flexible

As a beginning teacher, the challenge is to always find the right song for a given concept, subject, or theme. Veteran teachers have the opposite challenge: to not become rigid in their choices of songs or lessons. Become a lifelong learner, always willing to substitute and try something new in place of an old, familiar idea. Your students will pick up on this creativity, and it will help inspire them and keep you fresh and excited about teaching!

	Creative Sequence Lesson Plan with *Repertoire*
Grade/Class	Fourth-Fifth Grade
Date	February 2013
Primary Elemental Objective	**Style:** Sing an Anglo-American folk song, and trace it's origins and variations.
Secondary Elemental Objectives	**Melody:** Identify, sing, and play in *so* Pentatonic. **Rhythm:** Read and perform a song in cut time.
National/State Standard	NSME #1, 2, 3, 4, 5, 8, 9 P21 - Communication, Collaboration, Creativity
Repertoire	*The Golden Willow Tree*
Media	Singing Body Percussion Barred Percussion Recorder Speech (Dramatic)
Process - Explore - Analyze - Create	1. Sing the entire song, with verses, for the class, or play a recording. Ask the class to discuss the story. 2. Teach the shifting bass part by rote with text: "Sail on Willow Tree". Transfer to body percussion, then to barred percussion. Sing the song again over this soft accompaniment. Students should be able to pick up on the refrain "As she sailed on the Lowland..." and sing along. 3. Place the song notation on the board, or pass out song sheets. Using solfege, sight-read the melody together as a class. Identify the *so pentatonic* mode and vague *abba* phrase form (based on pitch ranges). 4. Identify letter names of notes in the song, and transfer to recorders. Give students plenty of time to practice, and review by phrases. 5. Create original phrases using small pitch sets (DEG, GAB, GAD) on recorder or barred percussion. Combine to make *abba* compositions/improvisations. 6. Return to mallet percussion and add melodic ostinato "Sailing high, sailing low". As a class, have students create a final form using song, recorders, mallet percussion, original tunes, and storytelling/acting. 7. Discuss the history behind the song. This song is an excellent example of the European/American folk tradition. The names of the ships have changed dozens of times. It may have started out as a song about Sir Walter Raleigh's ship "The Sweet Trinity", with the Lowland Sea referring to a shallow sea in Europe (Mediterranean, Irish Sea, Netherlands North Sea). The version here is an American variation, and talks about a ship sailing in South America! 8. Play recordings of the arrangements by Aaron Copland and Benjamin Britten. Discuss how a folk song is transformed into a performance piece by professional composers.
Assessments	1. Have the class write a short reflection while listening to Copland or Britten at the end of the lesson. 2. Assess improvisations based on phrase form, use of pitch sets, and rhythmic consistency.

There was a little ship in South Amerikee
'twas known by the name of the Golden Willow Tree
And she sailed on the lowlands, lonesome low
And she sailed on the lowland sea

Now she had not been sailing, not very long
For weeks not more than three
When she spied another ship all sailing low
And it was the Turkish Robberee

"Oh what shall I do, oh what shall I do?"
Our jolly well captain cried he
For we will all be sunk in the lowlands low
We'll be sunk in the lowland sea

Up steps a man to the captains side
"What will you give to me

If I sink her in the lowlands, lonesome low
If I sink her in the lowland sea?"

"Gold and lands I would give to thee
And also my daughter for to marry
If you sink her..."

Down he went to the briny sea
And swam beneath the Turkish Robberee
As it sailed ....

He cut and cut, one two three
And then swam back from the Turkish Robberee
And it sank in the lowlands...

"Only a fool would give gold and lands
And also his daughter to be at your command
You can drown in the lowlands...."

The Golden Willow Tree

Anglo-American Folk Song
Arranged by Tim Purdum

Arrangement Copyright 2009 by Tim Purdum.
All rights Reserved.

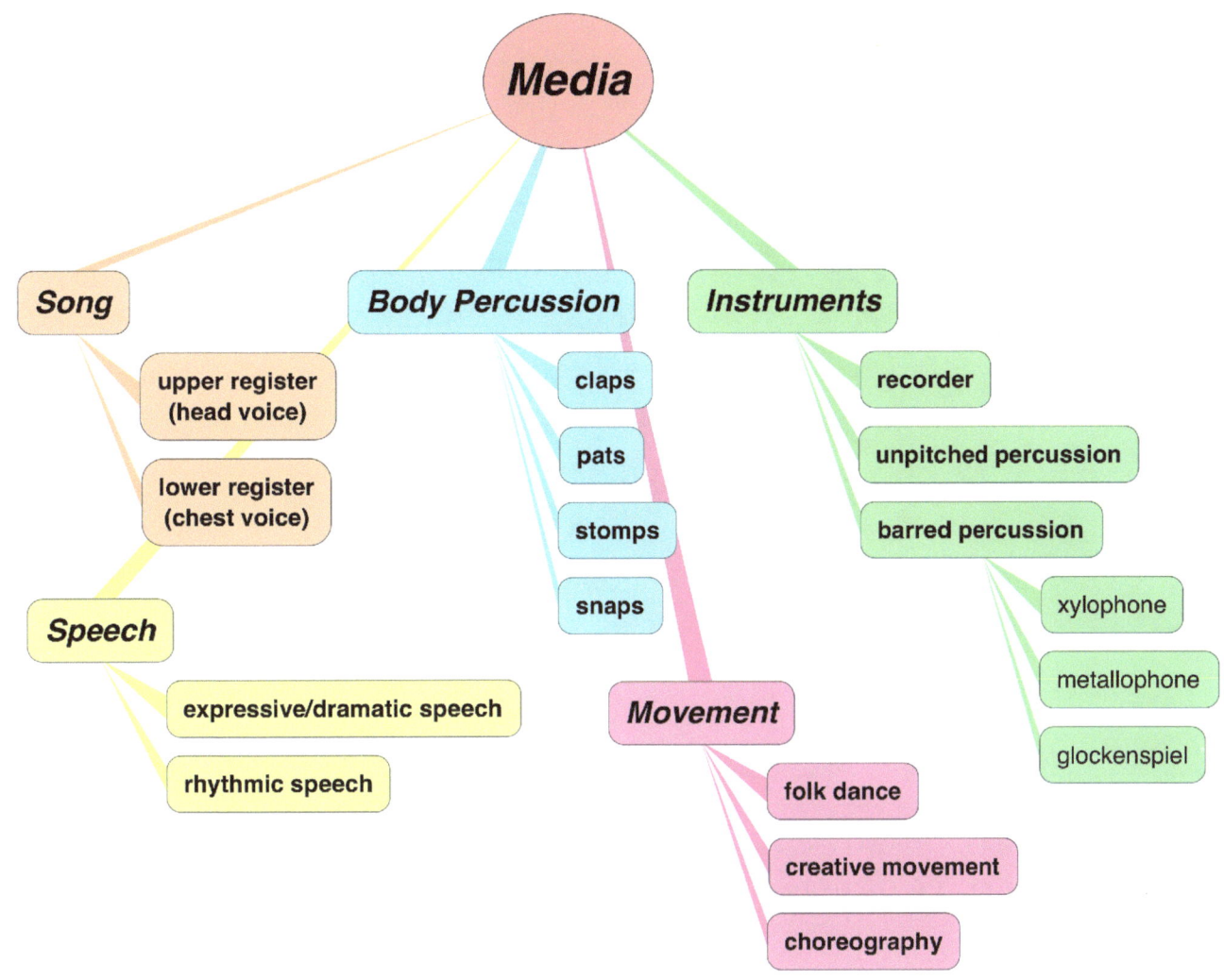

Media

The media are the vehicles through which students learn to make music. Elementary music classes are unfortunately often identified as "Vocal Music," and indeed, some teachers do little but teach singing. Yet through the use of expressive speech, percussion instruments, body percussion, and movement, students can truly explore the creative and collaborative aspects of music.

Speech

Speech is the link between music and language. Expressive use of one's voice is important for both singing and successful communication. Dramatic storytelling is a skill that all children should learn. Rhythmic speech has the advantage of isolating the rhythmic components of language. Poetry and Rap are both based on rhythmic speech, and are just as important artistically as melodic music. Choral reading reinforces rhythmic skills and speech fluency.

Song

By adding pitch to our expressive voice, we find that we were born with a melodic, flexible instrument! Song is the combination of melodic expression and linguistic expression. Unlike instrumental music, singing can quite literally tell a story, in words that everyone can understand, but with the added emotional and aesthetic impact of melodic and harmonic music.

Singing is also arguably the most important lifelong musical skill. Since it requires no equipment and is easy to do in a large group, singing can be the foundation of a return to community music making in this country, not just for children, but also for families, churches, and other social groups.

Body Percussion

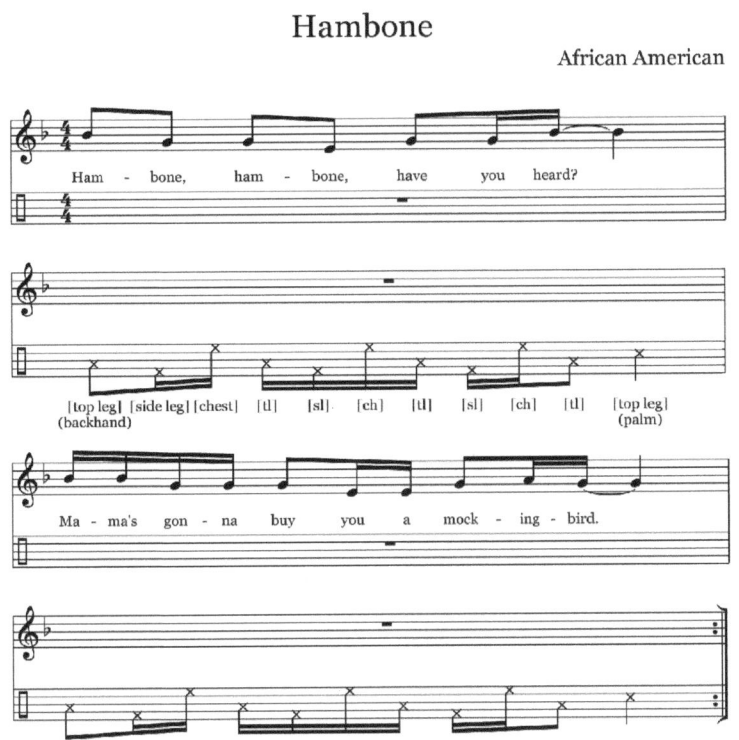

Hambone — African American

Another medium that we are born with is our body. Before learning to hit logs with sticks, primitive humans surely discovered that they could make rhythms with just their hands! Clapping, stomping, and patting knees give students a variety of simple ways to express themselves rhythmically. Snapping, while more advanced, is a challenging skill that students enjoy taking home and practicing. These four levels are only the beginning, however, and students can explore patting their shoulders, thumping their chests, rubbing their hands, or clapping with a partner.

Body percussion is its own unique art form, which has been taken to the professional level (Keith Terry is a modern performer) and developed into folk games (i.e., *hambone*, African-American body percussion). Gunild Keetman, Carl Orff's protégé, wrote an entire volume of body percussion exercises, titled *Rhythmische Übung*, published by Schott.

Instruments

Any musical instrument can of course have an important place in the music classroom. Yet there are sound arguments for using the combination of recorders, xylophones, and other percussion as the basis for making music together.

1. *Instruments should be available in quantity for classroom work.* Any time you have less than a 2:1 instrument to student ratio, the loss of instructional time while waiting turns has a big impact on the amount of material covered. Of course, a 1:1 ratio is ideal, but when sharing with a partner, this short wait time allows for reflection, observation, and cooperative learning, where students help each other.

2. *Instruments should be easy to learn and play.* Percussion instruments are really the simplest in terms of accessibility, since they are played primarily by large motor strikes. Small hand drums are light enough to be carried, and larger drums have stands to hold them. Classroom barred percussion are unique in that all of the bars are removable, allowing teachers to focus students on particular bars or scales, while removing "wrong" notes. Even the recorder, while more challenging than the percussion, is easy in comparison to other woodwind or brass instruments (not to mention a fraction of the cost).

3. *Instruments should support and enhance singing and movement.* Xylophones and other barred percussion have a mellow, light tone that can be used to accompany a song, without covering the children's singing voices. Recorder, when played properly, is also softer than other woodwinds. Also, the lightness of recorders, hand drums, and other percussion allow them to be used in conjunction with creative movement.

Many schools also utilize electric keyboards and/or guitars in their music classrooms. These instruments are excellent tools for teaching more advanced skills to students. They work particularly well in conjunction with studying chords and chord progressions. Electric keyboards have the challenge of a larger size, as well as power needs that make them less portable. They also are harder to play in a group, accompanying singing or dancing. Guitars, which work well as ensemble instruments, require more manual dexterity, and should be reserved for older students who are big enough to hold the instruments and coordinated enough to play. Despite their limits, both keyboards and guitars are inspiring for students, who can easily recognize and relate these instruments to performing groups that they see in multimedia.

Movement

Carl Orff, Émile Jaques-Dalcroze, and other leading music education experts incorporate movement and dance as integrated into learning music. While some "classically trained" music teachers are fearful of learning to include dance in their teaching, the joy on a child's face when they move aesthetically to music should be enough to overcome any objections.

1. *Movement and music are historically and culturally connected.* Throughout time and around the world, dance and music have existed simultaneously. From the winding street dances and improvisatory tunes of southern Europe and Latin America, to the graceful fluidity of Oriental theater and drumming, to the polyrhythmic drumming and stomping of west Africa, music and dance are one.
2. *Movement is a key tool for teaching rhythm, expression, and listening skills.* By moving to music, students are able to demonstrate their ability to keep a beat, follow a form, express a mood or style, and respond to cues. While all of these skills could theoretically be taught sitting at a desk, students are much more engaged by a movement-oriented lesson.
3. *Movement is a cross-disciplinary connection.* Both the National Standards and modern educational movements are pushing for more connections between music and other disciplines. Dance is one area that the music teacher can very easily demonstrate this connection.
4. *No one else will teach them to dance.* Like music, dance was once an integral part of the human experience. While a generation ago, physical education

teachers included square dances and other folk dances in their curricula, this has declined in recent years as their focus moves heavily toward the necessity to teach children physical fitness. It is disappointing that the state of the arts today in average public schools includes at most two classes, music and art. Drama, theater, and dance are not even on the radar of educational leaders, and art and music classes are constantly being pressured to do more with less time and resources, or being cut outright. By teaching dance (and drama) within the music curriculum, we are adding value to what we do as educators.

Movement can be broken into three categories:

Folk Dance

Like folk music, the dances of various times and cultures inform children about the world in ways they cannot learn in social studies class. Square Dances, Longways Sets, Circle Dances, Line Dances, and Snake Dances are just a few of the many forms that can be explored.

Creative Movement

Using the movement elements listed in the *Elements* chapter, students can explore their environment while listening to and responding to musical cues. This can begin with playful locomotor games, like skipping, galloping, and hopping. Eventually, students can create elaborate dance forms out of their own developed movement vocabulary.

Choreography

Choreography refers to composed dances. Just as some music is composed ahead of time and taught to children, so too can dances be written by the teacher or outside professional.

Chicken on a Fencepost

Traditional American

Chick-en on a fence-post, can't dance Jo-sie, chick-en on a fence-post, can't dance Jo-sie, Chick-en on a fence-post, can't dance Jo-sie, Hel-lo, Su-san Brown!

	Creative Sequence Lesson Plan with *Media*
Grade/Class	Fourth Grade
Date	November 2012
Primary Elemental Objective	**Rhythm:** Perform, identify, and create using sixteenth notes.
Secondary Elemental Objectives	**Melody**: Perform and create using *do* Pentatonic on F. **Style**: Play a traditional American children's circle game.
National/State Standard	NSME #1, 2, 3, 4, 5, 6 P21 - Collaboration, Creativity, Social Skills
Repertoire	*Chicken on a Fencepost*
Media	Singing Movement Speech Body Percussion Unpitched Percussion Barred Percussion
Process - Explore - Analyze - Create	1. Begin by having class stand in a circle, holding hands. Lead the class to walk 14 beats to the right around the circle. On beat 15, have them all raise their hands above their heads. Repeat the process, while teacher sings the song *Chicken on a Fencepost*. Identify the word cue for raising hands as "Brown." 2. Taking about a third of the class, create a smaller inner circle within the larger circle. Have this circle walk to the left while the outer circle walks to the right. 3. Assign "gates" - one set of arms in each circle that will raise on the word "Brown." All others now leave their arms down at end. After the song, walk through the gates to get to the center. Place a "chicken" object in the center of the circle. 4. Select two "farmers" to leave the circles and close their eyes. Choose two new gates, and begin the game again. At the end, the two farmers race to the center. The winner chooses the next two farmers, the loser chooses the next two gates. 5. After students have had a chance to play the game, ask them to sing the song. Have them pat or clap the rhythm of the words. Write the text on the board, and show them four rhythmic cards: quarter note, two eighth notes, four sixteenth notes, and quarter rest. Guide the class in pairing patterns with the text. Create a list of words for each pattern. 6. Echo-speak original patterns mixing up and playing with the text of the song (i.e., "brown, brown, chicken on a brown," "fencepost, Josie, Susan Brown.") 7. Using rhythm cards as a visual, have students in small groups compose original speech patterns of four beats. Add body percussion and/or unpitched percussion. Share each pattern with the class. 8. Compare patterns with the original song rhythm to identify parallel and complementary rhythms. Choose a pattern (or create a new one) that is highly complementary, and have it performed as an ostinato accompaniment to the song. 9. Move to the barred percussion, and set up in F-*do* Pentatonic (remove E and B bars). Teach melody of song by rote and/or with notation on the board, echoing each phrase. 10. While playing song, identify phrase form as *aa'ab*. Have students improvise a four-beat melodic pattern. 11. Students should now perform their improvisation three times in a row (*aaa*), and the teacher provides the fourth phrase (*b*). Switch roles, and have the teacher perform the *a* phrases and the students perform *b*. 12. Finally, have students create original songs using the entire *aaab* pattern. Share with the class. 13. Create an original arrangement using percussion ostinato, original song melody, and improvisations.
Assessments	1. Assess individuals or small groups on rhythmic pattern compositions. 2. Assess individuals on melodic improvisations. 3. Use review techniques or worksheets to assess understanding of sixteenth notes.

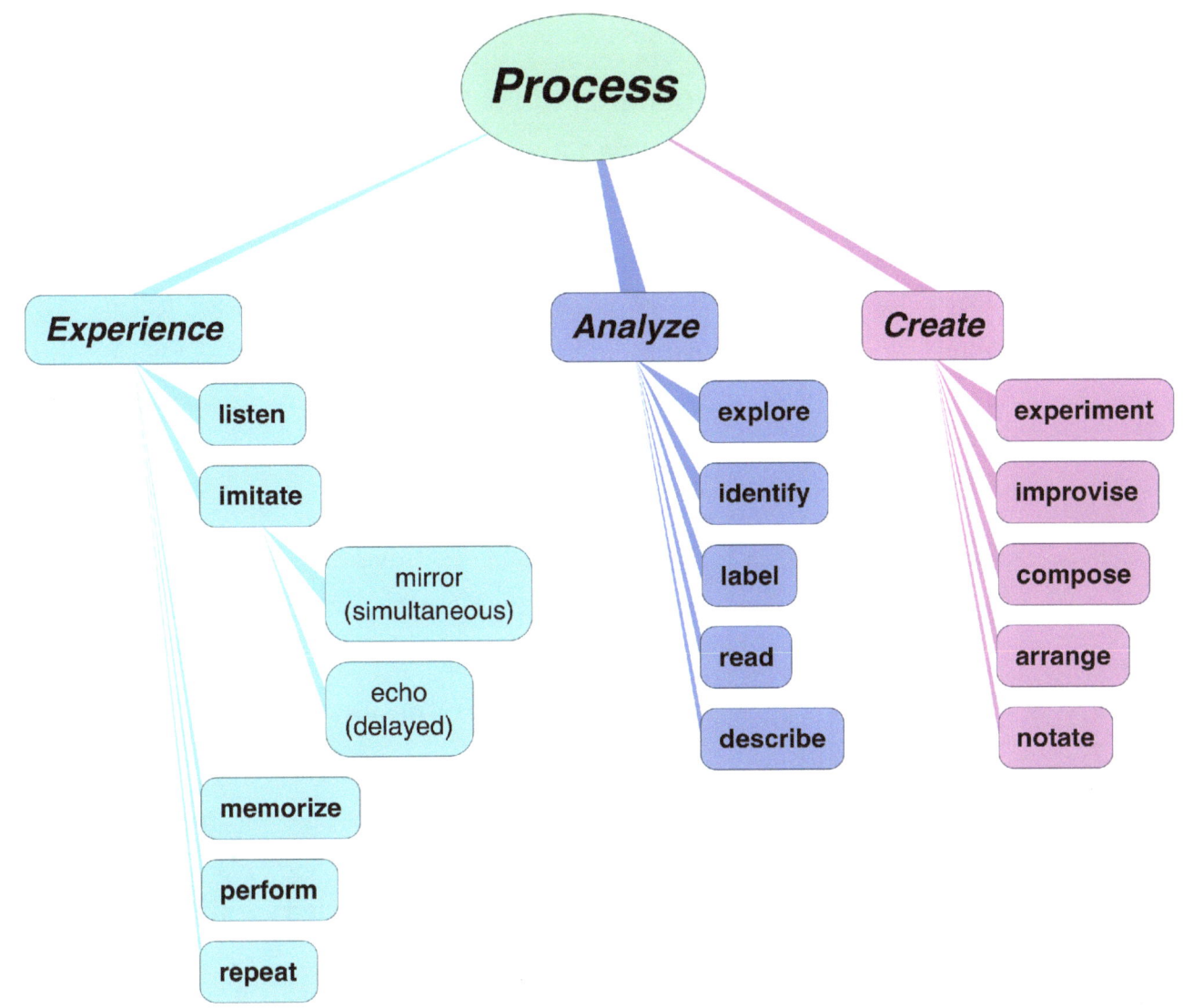

Process

Music education is a process. We are not looking to produce children who can replicate virtuosic performances without feeling. We do not seek to find the "talented" students, and encourage them at the expense of all others. Rather, we lead children on an exploratory journey through the *Elements* of music, using *Media* and *Repertoire*. There are many stages in this process, and they do not always follow in a clear sequence.

Experience

The first step in the process with young children involves *experiencing* the music. Students can listen to a model, then *imitate* that model. This delayed imitation is also known as *echo*. Simultaneous imitation can also sometimes be used, if the pattern or motion is simple enough. Students then *memorize*, *perform*, and *repeat* the musical pattern. Without this active experience, the child cannot fully *analyze* the music; nor can she *create* new musical patterns.

Analyze

Once students have been exposed to a new song, concept, or musical idea, they can begin to *explore* and *identify* elements within the music. Remember that in any objective, the performance concept comes before the symbol or notation. Only after they can identify a recurring concept are students ready to *label* this idea with a name and image.

Two new skills also flow directly from analysis. First, the student should now be able to *read* the newly introduced symbol, and recreate the appropriate concept. Second, students can now *discuss* this concept, through classroom discussion, one-on-one discussion, or written reflection. Reading and discussing become two important tools to assess the understanding and knowledge of students.

Create

Students who can *identify* a concept, even if unable to label it yet, can try using that concept in new ways. They might *experiment* with the order of rhythmic blocks, rearrange a melodic pattern, or tweak an accompaniment pattern to make it more complementary. Words can be substituted into a familiar song to create a new verse. The steps of a dance might be modified to add a hilarious ending.

Arrange

When larger decisions are made by students on the organization of a song or performance, they are *arranging* the piece. Arrangements can include adding an introduction or coda, writing accompaniment drones and ostinati, choosing instrumental voicing for different verses, etc. Graphic notation maps work well to document these decisions. This is an excellent way to include children in the creative process right before a performance, by allowing them to synthesize many different ideas that they have been exploring for weeks.

Improvise

If students take their experimentation a bit further, they may create completely new, spontaneous phrases of music. This is known as *improvisation*. Jazz musicians are famous for their improvised solos, but children can also learn to improvise. What is required are clear guidelines and plenty of practice.

Let's say a class is studying the pattern *mi-re-do*, and has just finished learning the sycopated pattern, ♪♩♪. The guidelines for an improvisation might be:

- 8 beat pattern
- Use only three bars A-G-F on barred percussion
- Change notes *slowly*, using plenty of repeated pitches
- Use syncopation at least once, all on one bar
- Maintain relationship with the steady beat
- End on *do* (F)

As you can imagine, every one of these criteria must first be experienced and identified through other activities. There should also be a large form to tie all of these individual performances together, such as a rondo, where each new solo is followed by a return to a familiar theme.

One simple way to introduce improvisation is through *Question & Answer*. Discuss the meaning of the terms with your class, pointing out that answers should relate to questions, and often use some of the same words, but rearranged in a new order. Use animal sounds, specific consonants, or other speech sounds to "scat" a question, and have the class give answers. Unlike an echo, the answer should not be identical to the question. Continue by having students perform Q&A patterns in pairs. This can be done with speech, scat singing, body percussion, or really any media, including movement.

Another improvisatory technique is to begin with a familiar *phrase form*, such as 'aaba'. Students can begin by playing/singing a familiar *a* phrase, and only improvising on the *b* phrase. Next, they can work on repeating a new, improvised *a* pattern three times. Finally, they put the two together to create a newly improvised piece with the whole form.

Compose

The difference between improvisation and composition is repetition. If a student tries to "perfect" the 'aaba' pattern mentioned above, trying out various ideas and finally settling on her favorite one, then she has moved into composition. Improvisation is at least partially spontaneous; it's never the same twice. Composition is planned, rehearsed, and performed. The same phrase forms and rondo structures used for improvisation work well to develop student compositions.

Students can expand on compositions using the same arranging skills they have already developed. Short phrase forms can become sections of larger works. Choreographed movement and carefully selected dynamics can add emotional impact to a performance. This is the ultimate assessment of a student's grasp on a concept - being able to apply it to a brand new work of art.

Notate

Once a composition is created, musical notation becomes an important tool for documenting, storing, and remembering the decisions that were made. This can be as simple as using rhythm cards or melodic noteheads to lay out a four-beat motive. Or it can include the use of staff paper, clefs, time signatures, barlines, etc. Older students can especially be motivated by the many software tools that are available to make notation look professional.

Notation can also include dictation exercises, where students must write down what they hear, or other worksheet-type activities. Yet just like with the English language, the most powerful motivator for a child to learn to write is to express herself.

The Flexibility of the Process

The creative process outlined in this chapter, like the musical *Elements* list, is *not* a step-by-step guide. Composition and notation often occur hand in hand, or prior to, labeling and reading. Students reviewing a familiar concept may not begin with experiential performance, but dive right into identifying and applying the ideas. Discussion and analysis can occur anytime throughout the process. Once again, the list is there to help you identify possibilities, connections, and areas where your students still need to go.

Ama Lama

American Playground Song

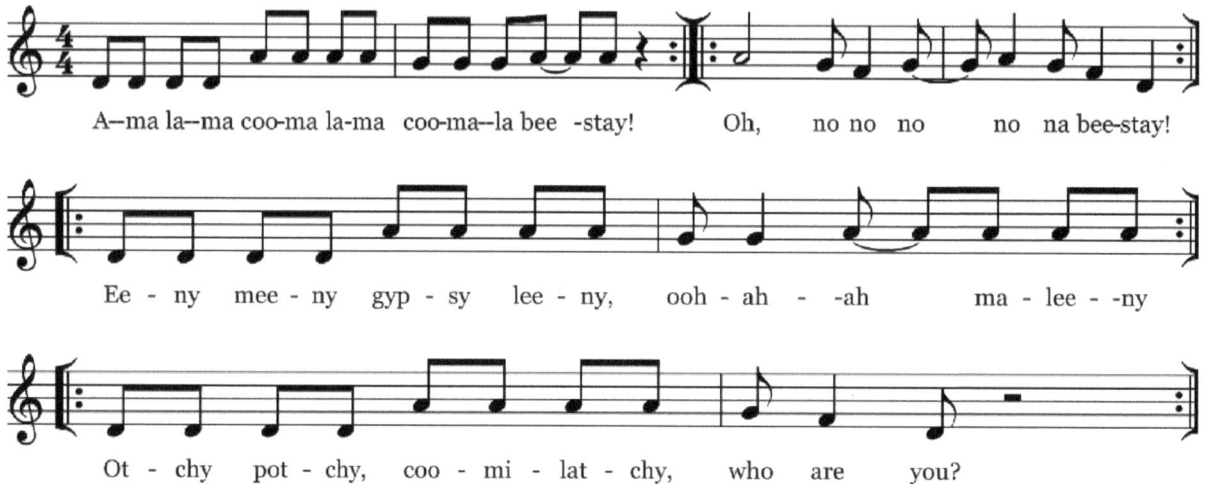

	Creative Sequence Lesson Plan with *Process* Based on a lesson by Roger Sams. Used with permission.
Grade/Class	Second-Fourth Grade
Date	January 2012
Primary Elemental Objective	**Form:** Use and identify *Question & Answer* (*Call & Response*) form.
Secondary Elemental Objectives	**Rhythm**: Improvise in a swing, jazz-style rhythm. **Timbre**: Explore expressive speech and singing through scat sounds and varied pitch.
National/State Standard	NSME #1, 3, 6, 7, 9 P21 - Creativity, Accountability, Innovation, Initiative & Self Direction
Repertoire	*Ama Lama*
Media	Singing Movement Speech Body Percussion

Process
- *Explore*
- *Analyze*
- *Create*
	Explore
	1. Write the following on the board. Point to it and speak, "Question, 2, 3, 4, 5, 6, 7, 8." See if the class can guess the second line ("Answer, 2, 3, 4, 5, 6, 7, 8.") Discuss what makes a question and an answer. Are they related? Give examples of good and bad conversations.
	
	    Q 2 3 4 5 6 7 8
	    A 2 3 4 5 6 7 8
	
	2. Tell the class a story about getting a flat tire out on the highway. You walk up to a farmhouse, but no one is home. In the barn, you see a lot of animals talking to each other!
	3. Give the class an example of an animal (i.e., chicken) asking a question, using the animal sounds rhythmically. Ask the class to give you an "answer" using some of the same sounds! Have the class suggest other animals. Remind students that the question and answer should not be identical.
	4. Continue the story: You walk outside of the barn and see a bright light in the sky. Suddenly, you are beamed up into a UFO, and taken on a journey around the galaxy. You travel to many different planets.
	5. Lead more Q&A examples, creating new alien languages for each new planet. Allow students to suggest new planets/languages.
	6. Finish story: the aliens finally bring you home, but before dropping you off, they teach you a song!
	7. Teach the class "Ama Lama" by echo-singing each phrase.
	Create
	1. Have the class stand up and walk around the room while singing. Encourage them to walk like a barn animal, or an alien! At the end of the song, they should face a nearby partner.
	2. With partners, have students take turns asking questions and giving answers to the beat. Each questioner gets to choose the language.
	3. Return to the song and travel around, finding a new partner.
	4. Expand the game by replacing the speech with singing voices and/or body percussion Q&A.
	Analyze
	1. Introduce the concept of "Scat" singing to the class. Play them an example (i.e., *Mumbles Returns* by Clark Terry). Discuss similarities with the *Ama Lama* game.
	2. Identify and discuss swing beat underlying jazz songs and *Ama Lama*. Add a ride cymbal to performances of the song and game: "car, park the car..."
	3. Continue exploring and learning about jazz in future lessons.

Assessments	Take time to hear Q&A partners perform. Assess on ability to create within the confines of the 8 beat phrase.

Synthesizing, Organizing and Writing Lesson Plans

Synthesizing the *Elements*, *Repertoire*, *Media*, and *Process* into a coherent lesson planning strategy requires patience, consistency, and yes, creativity!

The first step in planning is to fill out the *Elemental Concepts Map* found at the end of the *Elements* chapter. This gives you a full set of concepts that spans all grades in your program. Begin by taking the bubble chart of each Element in this book, and deciding what you want to add, remove, or keep the same. You can also be thinking generally about the sequence in which these concepts are taught as you write them down.

Creative Sequence
Yearly Map of Elemental Music Concepts (Sample)

	Rhythm	Melody	Harmony	Form	Timbre	Expression	Style
Kdg	Beat Fast vs. Slow Sound vs. Silence Word rhythms	High vs. Low Matching pitch Upper register (head voice)	Steady beat Tonic drone	Same vs. Different AB phrase	Male/Female voices Children's voices High/Low register Classroom instruments	Loud vs. Soft Short vs. Long Expressive speech Movement vocabulary	American/European nursery rhymes & folk songs March Lullaby
1st	Quarter note Quarter rest Eighth notes	*so-mi* *la-so-mi* staff treble clef	Chord drone (open fifth) Broken drone Rhythmic ostinato	ABA Motive aaba (phrase form) Call & Response (Q&A) Ostinato Repeat signs	Guitar Piano Banjo Ukelele	*piano* *forte* Smooth vs. separated	American folk (including African-Am.) European folk
2nd	Tie Half note Half rest Whole note Whole rest Compound division	*mi-re-do* Pentatonic scale (F=do)	Level drone 2-part round Melodic ostinato	abab aabb aaab	Percussion (world)	*crescendo* *decrescendo*	African folk Latin American folk
3rd	Dotted half note Dotted half rest Meters of 2, 3, 4 (simple & compound) 2/4, 3/4, 4/4 time signatures Offbeat	Transposition Pentatonic scale (C=do), (G=do) la Pentatonic (E, D, A)	Partner songs Crossover drone (fifth and octave) Moving drone 3-part round Layered ostinati	Rondo	Winds (world)	*staccato* *legato* *mezzo-piano* *mezzo-forte* *pianissimo* *fortissimo*	Asian folk Australian folk Waltz
4th	Syncopation Sixteenth notes Eighth rest Eighth/Sixteenth combinations	*re* Petatonic *so* Pentatonic *do* Hexatonic *la* Hexatonic Ionian (major) Aeolian (minor)	4-part round Parallel thirds I-ii chords (major) i-VII chords (minor)	Theme & Variations Sonata Allegro	Orchestra Orchestral families	Largo Andante Allegro accent	Medieval Renaissance Baroque Classical Romantic 20th Century
5th	Compound time 6/8 time signature	Dorian (re) Phrygian (mi) Lydian (fa) Mixolydian (la)	I-IV-V chords (major) 12 bar blues	Verse & Chorus Bridge Intro Coda	Electronics	tenuto fermata rubato	Blues Jazz Rock & Roll Country Rap Hip-Hop Pop

Creative Sequence
Yearly Map of Elemental Music Concepts

	Rhythm	Melody	Harmony	Form	Timbre	Expression	Style
Kdg							
1st							
2nd							
3rd							
4th							
5th							

Yearly Goals

Once you have chosen the basic scope of your curriculum, you are ready to break this up into grade-level goals. On the *Yearly Map* above, divide your Elemental concepts into goals for each grade to achieve *this year*. Note that if you are beginning a new program or at a new school, there can and should be quite a bit of overlap between grades. Even in well established programs, certain fundamental goals like matching pitch and keeping a steady beat should probably appear in more than one grade. Set high but reasonable goals for your students. It's OK to not achieve all of these goals, but you'll feel better if you get close. You may have advanced goals on your *Elemental Concepts Map* that you realize your older students will not achieve the first year. This is why priorities are so important as you work. Rather than rushing through material to "cover" difficult concepts, plan to take time and make sure fundamental skills are sound.

Monthly Planning Calendar

Next, we must look at the scope of the year, and take into account all of the events that occur from fall to spring. Using the *Planning Calendar* below, first mark down all performances, assemblies, holidays, field trips, and other school events that you are aware of that will impact your teaching schedule. As new events are scheduled, be sure to add them to your calendar. If you keep this calendar up to date throughout the year, you will be better able to foresee those weeks or months where your teaching of new concepts is going to be limited due to time and responsibilities.

After marking down these obligations, begin penciling in your *priority* concepts. This should be four to six big, key items that you feel this class *must* learn *this* year. They should also be the goals that are able to be assessed for report cards. Take an estimate on how much time you need to truly *process* each concept, not just introduce it. Remember, students must first *Experience* the concept, then they can

Analyze and *Create* using that concept. When you have your priorities set, stop there. Don't copy down every single concept from the *Yearly Map* yet.

Next, go through your repertoire collection and choose at least one piece of music, dance, game, or activity per month, to explore, teach, and reinforce each priority concept. Write them into your calendar. Now, look to see what *secondary* concepts these pieces can cover. Don't worry if they weren't on your original yearly list! Unless you feel the skill or concept is too difficult, you can always include it when it comes up in the repertoire. Add these secondary concepts below each piece.

Finally, go back and pencil in any additional concepts, repertoire, and other secondary goals that will help fill out the year and make sense in the progression you have created. Do not overfill the Planning Calendar with every possible concept for the year. Rather, begin with the priority ideas, and see where other concepts can fit in as the year progresses.

					Creative Sequence Planning Calendar (Sample)					
3rd Grade	Aug.	Sept.	Oct.	Nov.	Dec.	Jan.	Feb.	Mar.	Apr.	May
Events	Sch. Starts 8/12	Labor Day 9/2	Hallowe'en 10/31	Thanksgiving 11/22	Concert 12/12 Winter Break 12/20-		Valent. Day 2/14	Spr. Break 3/12-20	Concert 4/23	Last Day 5/31
Priority Concepts	Review basic rhythms & pitches	Pentat. Scale in F, C, G	---	Meter of 3, 3/4 Time Sign.	---	African American Music	---	Recorder tonguing breathing G-E	---	---
Repertoire		*John Kanaka*	*Ghost of John*	*Derry Ding Dong Dason*; Tinikling	Snow & Ice word chant; *Jingle Bells*; *The North Wind Doth Blow*	*Head & Shoulders Baby 123*; *Ama Lama*		*Rain Rain Go Away*; *May Flowers*	Spring Theme(?) for Concert	Comp. Projects
Secondary Concepts		Syncop. ♪♩♪ Dotted Quarter	Legato Staccato *piano forte*	English Music; Phillipino Dance	*abab'* Mmvt. vocab: slip, slide, glide, fall, blow	Offbeat; Q&A Improv.	Folk Dances: Longways Set			Apply staff notation A/V recording

Creative Sequence
Planning Calendar

3rd Grade	Aug.	Sept.	Oct.	Nov.	Dec.	Jan.	Feb.	Mar.	Apr.	May
Events										
Priority Concepts										
Repertoire										
Secondary Concepts										

Rewriting the Maps

Keep a paper or digital copy of your *Elemental Concepts Map*, *Yearly Map*, and *Planning Calendar* where you can access them, refer to them, and rewrite them throughout the year. No one can truly predict how long students will need or want to explore a given concept. We can enforce a limit on this time, but often it serves the class better to let them have *more* time to experience, analyze, and create at a deeper level. We also cannot always predict the flashes of intuition that help us and our students create processes. As the year progresses, mark changes to the sequence, priorities, concepts and repertoire, first on the *Planning Calendar*. By the end of the year, revisit the *Yearly Map* and *Essential Concepts Map* and update these to reflect what you have learned about your students, your situation, music education in general, and your own personal teaching style. If you are not reviewing this curriculum at least yearly and tweaking processes and repertoire for the following year, it will get stale, predictable and become less effective.

Writing Lesson Plans

While some teachers write a lesson plan for every class period, these documents often don't show the consistent flow from day to day, or the overarching goals that can take weeks to achieve. Begin instead by writing a lesson plan for your *priority Elemental objectives*, detailing all the *Repertoire, Media*, and steps in the *Process* you plan to use to achieve that goal, as well as secondary Elemental concepts that will come into play. This lesson plan may then be used for a week, a month, or longer. It also is, once again, only a guideline, not a strict series of steps. After each attempt at teaching part of the lesson, sit down and reflect on what is working, not working, and can be improved. Big changes can then be added back into the lesson.

Textbook series often call these bigger lesson plans Units, where the focus is drawn heavily toward one particular aspect of music. The difference in a **Creative Sequence** lesson plan is that there should be a constant flow between objectives, repertoire, media, and process. As you teach your main objective, new secondary concepts will arise and be addressed. Given the length of some music periods, you may even decide to be running two different lesson plans simultaneously, and discover ways in which the different repertoire and concepts overlap.

The example lesson provided in this chapter illustrates how inter-connected the sequence of objectives becomes. Despite a clear goal of learning about and identifying 6/8 time, the two pieces used could just as easily lead to a serious study of major and minor scales. While we wrote this in as a secondary objective, it would also make sense to then continue with scales as the primary objective for the next large lesson, and use these two examples as starting points.

Writing Elemental Objectives

It may seem that we have already done this work, in our multiple maps and planners. Yet these charts really only highlight key *concepts*. What is needed in the lesson plan is a student-oriented *objective*, written in a complete sentence, that is clear and specific. Begin each objective with the phrase "Students will..." either written in or implied. Think about the specific skill or knowledge that you wish your students to be able to demonstrate by the end of the lesson.

Secondary objectives are those that fit nicely into the lesson, but are not your main goal. All songs, for example, have rhythm, melody, and probably a recognizable form. As a secondary objective, then, you can point out that your students are *experiencing* this element, even if they do not *analyze* or *create* using the element. This allows you to build your next lesson knowing that your students have already had this experience, and are ready to further process that particular element.

	Creative Sequence Lesson Plan (sample)
Grade/Class	Fifth Grade
Date	September 2012
Primary Elemental Objective	**Rhythm**: Explore, improvise, identify, and compose in compound meter & 6/8 time.
Secondary Elemental Objectives	**Melody**: Explore the Diatonic Major (Ionian) and Minor (Aeolian) scales. **Form**: Improvise in Q&A form using hand drums. **Harmony**: Compose and perform rhythmic ostinati.
National/State Standard	NSME #1, 2, 3, 4, 5, 6 P21 - Creativity, Productivity, Flexibility, Collaboration
Repertoire	*Girls & Boys Come Out to Play* *To Work Upon the Railway*
Media	Singing Speech Clapping Hand Drums Barred Percussion Movement
Process - Explore - Analyze - Create	1. Sing the song *Girls & Boys* for your class. Ask them to retell the story in their own words. 2. Break the song into two-line sections, and have groups of students create pantomime performances acting out the words while you sing. 3. Ask the class to sing along. Use printed text and echoing to reinforce learning. 4. While singing, have the class find the beat and pat it on their knees. Next, have them get up and march to the beat. Have them explore and try out different ways of moving to the song. Identify skipping and galloping as two motions that fit well. 5. Return to circle/seats. Have students transfer skipping pattern back to their hands, clapping. Lead echo-claps of 4 beat patterns, using 1, 2, and 3 claps on each beat (still in compound meter of the song). 6. Lead a *Question & Answer* pattern of 8 beats, with the class answering by copying part of your original pattern. Next, have them turn to a neighbor and take turns leading. Maintain the beat by accompanying on a drum. 7. Turn the song into a game: class skips while singing, then finds a partner to do Q&A with after each verse. Extend game by having class use hand drums for Q&A. 8. Place four cards with words and rhythms out for the class to see, in a mixed up order: *oo-ree* *ay* *oo-ree* *fillimee* 9. Sing the song *To Work Upon the Railway* to the class. Have them decide what order to place the cards in. 10. Teach this pattern, the chorus, to the class. Have them sing the chorus while you sing the verse. 11. Lead a discussion on time signatures and meters. Point out that despite the strange collections of notes on the cards, each card feels like one beat of music. 12. Introduce 6/8 time signature. Discuss how the numerals point to 6 eighth notes per measure, but that this isn't the beat that we feel because of the speed of the song. 13. In small groups, let the students explore composing new patterns using the rhythm cards, and sharing with the class. 14. Show the class notation of *Girls & Boys*. Identify the time signature as 6/8, and meter as compound.
Assessments	1. Photograph the notation and/or record a performance of the student's group compositions in 6/8 time. 2. Give a quick worksheet where students must identify compound and simple time examples by listening. 3. Take turns clapping improvised patterns in 6/8, and assess each performance based on a rhythmic rubric.

Girls & Boys Come Out to Play
Traditional English

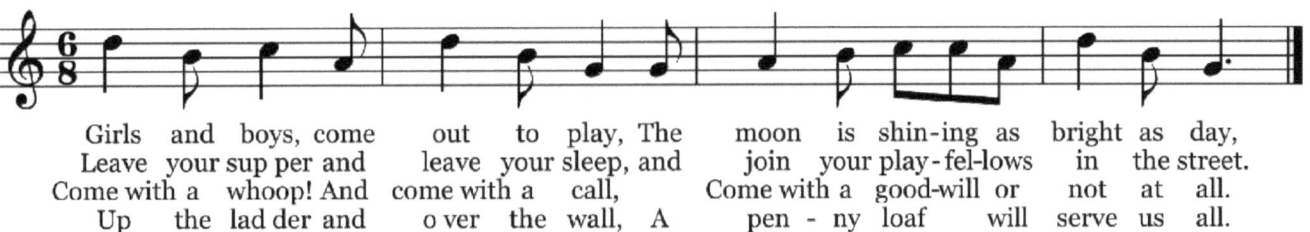

Girls and boys, come out to play, The moon is shin-ing as bright as day,
Leave your sup per and leave your sleep, and join your play-fel-lows in the street.
Come with a whoop! And come with a call, Come with a good-will or not at all.
Up the lad der and o ver the wall, A pen - ny loaf will serve us all.

To Work Upon the Railway
Irish American

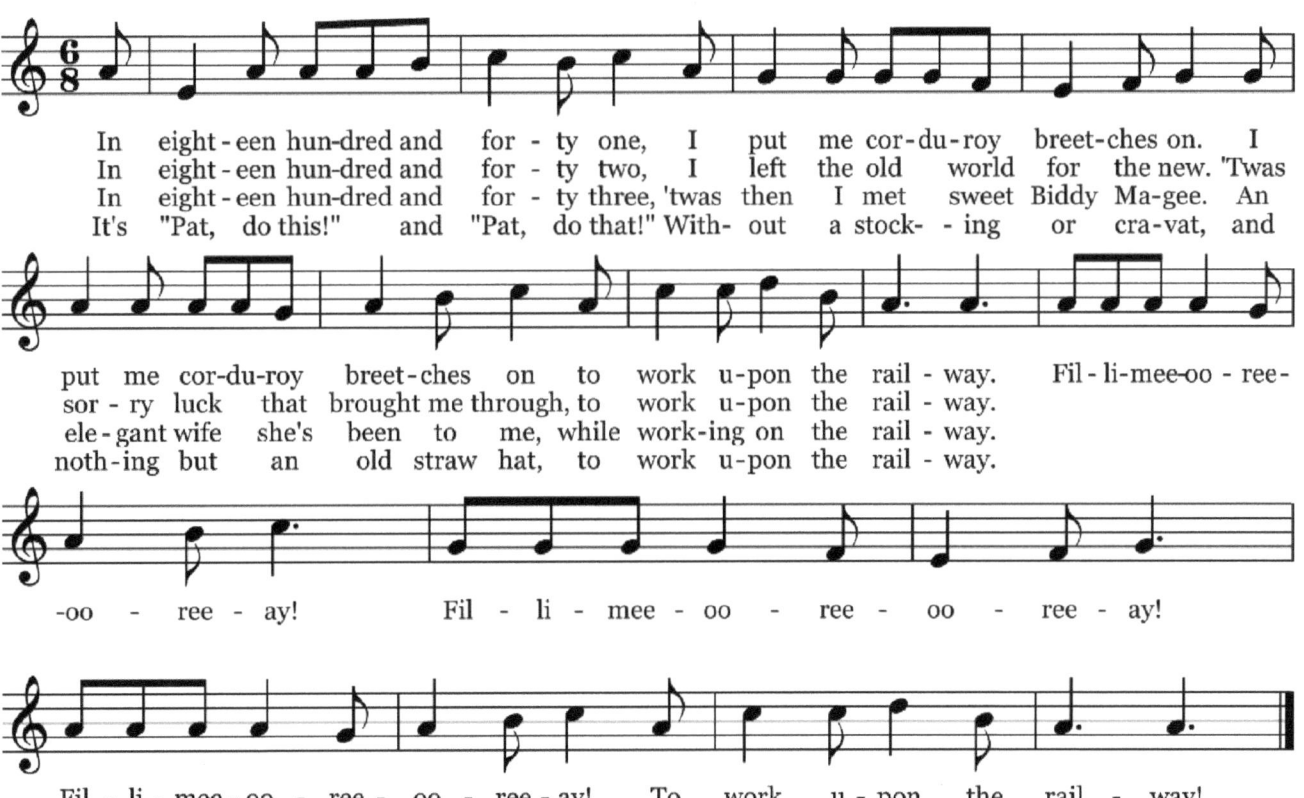

In eight-een hun-dred and for - ty one, I put me cor-du-roy breet-ches on. I
In eight-een hun-dred and for - ty two, I left the old world for the new. 'Twas
In eight-een hun-dred and for - ty three, 'twas then I met sweet Biddy Ma-gee. An
It's "Pat, do this!" and "Pat, do that!" With- out a stock- - ing or cra-vat, and

put me cor-du-roy breet-ches on to work u-pon the rail - way. Fil - li-mee-oo - ree-
sor - ry luck that brought me through, to work u-pon the rail - way.
ele - gant wife she's been to me, while work-ing on the rail - way.
noth-ing but an old straw hat, to work u-pon the rail - way.

-oo - ree - ay! Fil - li - mee - oo - ree - oo - ree - ay!

Fil - li - mee - oo - ree - oo - ree - ay! To work u - pon the rail - way!

	Creative Sequence **Lesson Plan**
Grade/Class	
Date	
<u>Primary Elemental Objective</u>	
Secondary Elemental Objectives	
National/State Standard	
<u>Repertoire</u>	
<u>Media</u>	
<u>Process</u> - *Explore* - *Analyze* - *Create*	
Assessments	

Daily Planner

The *Daily Planner*, or lesson book, is the place to keep track of the lesson process. A short list of repertoire and process steps, written down in a small square each day, allows you to quickly check before, during, and after a class. You can track your progress by simply checking off pieces of the lesson that went well, jotting down creative extensions that arise, and then writing in the next steps for the following day. Do not try to recreate your entire lesson plan in the *Daily Planner*. Rather, keep it very concise, simple, and easy to read at a glance.

Creative Extensions

With a well-planned lesson based on sequential, age-appropriate objectives, you can begin each class knowing that you are prepared to teach your students to the best of your ability. However, *do not let the lesson plan interfere with student creativity*! Whenever possible, recognize creative ideas when they occur, and allow your students and yourself the opportunity to pursue these ideas. You must find balance between meeting the established curricular expectations and allowing the *Process* to truly happen naturally. Too often we move on to a new activity or focus just when students are beginning to understand and want to explore the previous concepts.

	Monday	Tuesday	Wednesday	Thursday	Friday
Creative Sequence **Daily Planner**					
1st Class					
2nd Class					
3rd Class					
4th Class					
5th Class					
6th Class					
7th Class					
8th Class					

Assessment

The push for assessment in modern education is both a blessing and a curse for the music educator. The challenge lies in finding authentic, practical ways to assess and document musical knowledge and skills, without taking time away from our already limited contact with students, or turning music class into another mind-numbing, paper-pencil testing site for children. The promise of assessment is in the recognition of music and the arts as a core component of a 21st century education. By seeking to avoid assessment requirements, music teachers sometimes reinforce the stereotypes of music as a "fluff" course, that can then be easily eliminated when budgets get tight.

The good news is that, by following the creative process, you are already continually assessing your students.

Perform *Hot Cross Buns* on Barred Percussion	Mallet Technique: proper hold, position, alternating hands 1 - Unable to hold 2 - 3 - Basic grip and position are good, some issues alternating 4 - 5 - Good grip, position, and alternating of hands	Rhythmic Accuracy: Tempo, steadiness 1 - No sense of pulse 2 - 3 - Basic relationships are evident, but tempo is not steady 4 - 5 - Excellent pulse, tempo, and rhythm	Pitch Accuracy: Correct pattern of notes 1 - Unrecognizable melodic pattern 2 - 3 - Basic melodic structure is correct, 1-2 mistakes in pattern 4 - 5 - Correct melodic pattern
Johnny	4	5	3
Kaitlyn	2 (all one hand)	5	5
Alex	5	2 (all on beat, no rhythm)	4
Sam	3	5	5
Josie	5	4	5
Elliot	4	5	4

Performance Assessment

Every time they perform a pattern, we listen, analyze, and give feedback, which the students then use to improve. This is informal assessment. In order to document this assessment, create a simple rubric of the expectations, and check off each student according to their performance. This is not necessary to do daily or weekly, but by documenting performance on priority concepts, you have the necessary information to show parents, administrators, and improve student learning.

Composition/Portfolio Assessment

When a student composes a new ostinato, melody, or rhythm, and notates it or records it, you now have a document for a student portfolio to show accomplishment and growth. Notation does not have to be pencil and paper. It could use manipulatives like rhythm cards or noteheads. Quick photographs of the cards can then document the pattern. Older students should learn to make note symbols and write on a staff, but this can also be aided by computer notation software. Finally, making an audio or video recording of a student or group composition can also document the learning.

Creating a digital portfolio for each student in your class is a great way to organize all of these documents, videos, and recordings. Depending on where your school and parents are with technology, it may become necessary to print out or put the files on CD to share them with families.

Reflection Papers

Throughout the year, you should be having class discussions on various topics, to informally assess the understanding that students have for particular concepts. After students perform a concert or see a performance, have them spend a short time actually writing a reflection of what they observed and learned. This should be done only a few times a year, to not take away too much music-making time. Put the reflection into the student portfolio.

Report Cards

Whatever the format of your school's report cards, it is often up to the teacher to decide what actual assessments and goals will be listed, or used to calculate the grade. Begin with your priority concepts for the year, and make assessments (such as the three types listed above) based on these goals the focus of the report card. By integrating this requirement with the learning process, the report cards will be valid and accurate, without costing your children valuable on-task learning time.

Report Card 2012 Music Class Mr. Purdum			
Name	Elliot		
Grade	First		
M = Meets Expectation PM = Partially Meets Expectation NM = Does Note Meet Expectation N/A = Not Assesssed Yet	**First Term**	**Second Term**	**Third Term**
Performance Assessment: Read & perform rhythms using quarter notes, eighth notes, and quarter rests.	M	- -	- -
Performance Assessment: Read & sing three-note melodies with accurate pitch in the upper register.	PM (not always matching pitch)	M	- -
Composition: Create and notate a four-beat rhythm pattern.	N/A	M	- -
Composition: Write and notate a short melodic phrase.	N/A	N/A	M
Reflection Writing: Create a story through words and drawings based on a recorded piece of music.	N/A	N/A	M
Behavior & Participation	M	M	M
Note:	See attached examples of student work.		

Creative Sequence and the NAfME National Standards

Elements	Repertoire	Media	Process
Literacy Skills *Performance Skills*	*Cross-Discipline Connections* *Cultural & Historical Knowledge*	*Performance Skills*	*Creative Skills* *Literacy Skills* *Analytical Skills*
NS #5 - Reading and notating music	NS #8 - Understanding relationships between music, the other arts, and disciplines outside of the arts	NS #1 - Singing, alone and with others, a varied repertoire of music	NS #3 - Improvising melodies, variations, and accompaniments
	NS #9 - Understanding music in relation to history and culture	NS #2 - Performing on instruments, alone and with others, a varied repertoire of music	NS #4 - Composing and arranging music within specified guidelines
			NS #6 - Listening to, analyzing, and describing music
			NS #7 - Evaluating music and music performaces

The National Association for Music Education (NAfME), previous MENC, wrote National Standards for Music Education in 1994. These standards provide a big-picture view of music education. Goals are set by grade span, K-4, 5-8, & 9-12. Standards include singing, playing instruments, reading and notating music, improvising, composing, analyzing music, evaluating music, and connecting music to other disciplines, history, and culture. The nine standards are broad, excellent descriptors of *what students should be able to do*. Yet there are several drawbacks to this design.

1. *Elements of music are broken across seven standards, and not detailed in any of them.* Unlike the Elements chapter of this book, or the curriculum printed in most textbooks, the National Standards do not go into much detail on rhythm, melody, harmony, etc. There are bullet points under each standard, but they are just a few sentences long.

2. *Elements are tied closely to notation.* The bullet points that do address rhythmic patterns and other elemental concepts are primarily under NS #5 - *Reading and Notating Music*. This unfortunately reinforces the concept that the goal of music class is to learn notation, rather than the goal of learning notation is to help you learn to make music.
3. *Body Percussion, Speech, and Movement are excluded as creative musical media.* By focusing primarily on singing (NSME #1) and playing instruments (NSME #2), the National Standards ignore other creative ways to make and respond to music.
4. *The NSME are too broad to be particularly useful in planning a curriculum.* Because of their national nature and attempts to meet diverse needs, the writing teams for the NSME wrote guidelines that help describe what we teach to outsiders, but do not really impart a lot of insight to new music educators.

Regardless of their shortcomings, it is important for music educators to be able to document how their work aligns with the National Standards for Music Education. As you can see by the chart, by following a **Creative Sequence** with your children, you will achieve all nine standards in an organic, balanced way.

Currently, the NSME are being rewritten, by NAfME and a consortium of arts education groups. Also, many state standards have been written based on the NSME. For up-to-date information on aligning **Creative Sequence** with state and national standards, please visit cedarrivermusic.com/cs/standards.

Creative Sequence and 21st Century Skills

	P21 Skills	*Creative Sequence*
Learning and Innovation Skills	Creativity and Innovation	***Process***: Create Compose, Improvise, Arrange
	Critical Thinking and Problem Solving	***Process***: Analyze & Create Listen, Describe, Analyze, Compose, Arrange
	Communication and Collaboration	***Process***: Experience, Analyze, & Create Imitate, Perform, Listen, Identify, Describe, Arrange, Compose (group projects)
Life and Career Skills	Flexibility and Adaptability	***Process***: Create Improvise, Arrange, Compose
	Initiative and Self-Direction	***Process***: Create Improvise, Compose, Arrange (independent projects)
	Social and Cross-Cultural Skills	***Repertoire***: World Folk Music ***Process***: Experience, Analyze Imitate, Perform, Listen, Describe
	Productivity and Accountability	***Process***: Analyze, Create, & Experience Read, Notate, Compose, Arrange, Perform
	Leadership and Responsibility	***Process***: Create Compose, Arrange (group projects)

In addition to national and state music standards, **Creative Sequence** can be easily tied to cross-curricular skills, demonstrating the essential and central role that music plays in a whole-child curriculum. The *Partnership for 21st Century Skills* (www.p21.org) is one organization that seeks to standardize these holistic, multi-disciplinary skills. In addition to traditional "Core Subjects" (which include the Arts), and information/technology skills, P21 lists two categories of skills that can be closely tied to the music curriculum:

- *Learning and Innovation Skills*
- *Life and Career Skills*

The chart above illustrates how easily the creative *Process* can align with these goals. By defining our teaching based on 21st Century goals, we move music from a peripheral, enrichment subject to a core component of a 21st Century education. It is imperative of every arts educator to learn to speak this language when talking with administrators, parents, legislators, and the community at large. News from around the country tells us that music and other arts are in danger of being eliminated in many districts, thanks to inadequate funding and an increased focus on high-stakes testing. Music teachers must become advocates, both locally and nationally, for the whole-child education that we know we must be moving towards this century.

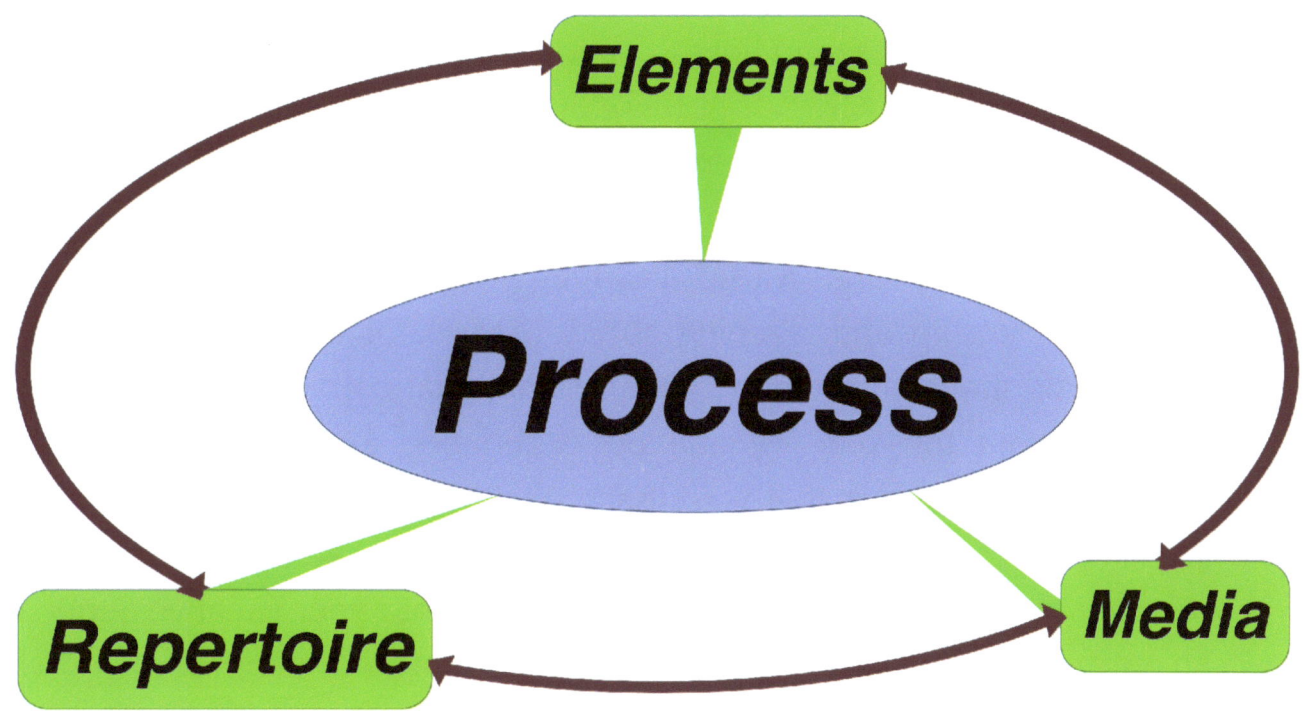

Moving Forward with Creative Sequence and Your Classroom

The Creative Sequence is created by you, based on the needs for your students and situation. You must discover, through planning, practice, and reflection, the best way to teach essential performance skills (*Media*), traditional songs (*Repertoire*) and musical concepts (*Elements*) to your classes. The creative *Process* allows you to actively engage students as music makers, composers, and arrangers. Do not settle for merely training your students to be a good audience that knows how to appreciate a professional performance. Remember, *all children can and should learn to make music*!

Where to go from here?

1. *Begin (or continue) collecting resources*: Find books, websites, and other sources that provide repertoire and process ideas for you to incorporate into your classes. At *cs.cedarrivermusic.com*, you can find a variety of resources to

continue your journey, including a searchable repertoire database, future supplemental publications, and links to various other online resources.
2. *Map out your next year*: Give all of these concepts in this book a try, and keep track of what is working, and what needs to be revised for the following year.
3. *Seek out workshops and training*: Summer courses in Orff Schulwerk, Kodály, Dalcroze-Eurhythmics, and Music Learning Theory will all advance your personal musicianship and teaching abilities. Many of these approaches also have local workshops and state, regional, or national conferences that you can attend throughout the year. When you experience a new approach, don't immediately dismiss things that you disagree with. Rather, discover the reasons behind the differences in these philosophies, and explore what is truly important in your own teaching. Incorporate what you learn into your Creative Sequence as you go!
4. *Share what you know*: Give back to the music education community by sharing resources with your colleagues. Whether it be pointing out a book like this to a friend, or writing up your own new lesson and sharing it at a workshop, beginning to teach other teachers is an excellent way to assess how well you truly understand your subject matter.
5. *Continue to love and teach children*: Keep focused on what is important. Stay balanced between work and home life. Demonstrate your love of music to your students. Inspire them to help build a world that is full of song, where people from any corner of the globe can hold hands and dance together!

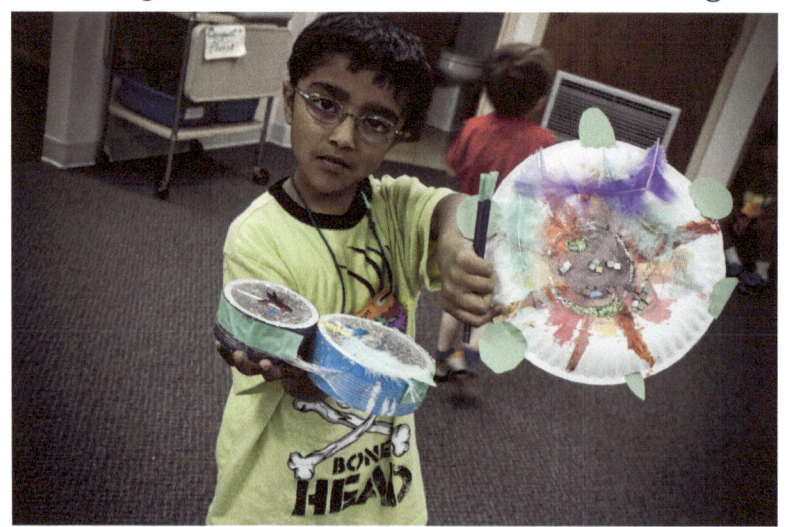

Resources & References

<u>Books</u>

150 American Folk Songs to sing, read, and play, ed. Peter Erdei, Boosey & Hawkes, 1974.

Goodkin, Doug. *Nows the Time: Teaching Jazz to All Ages*, Pentatonic Press, 2004.

Keetman, Gunild and Carl Orff. *Music for Children, Vol. I-V,* ed. Margaret Murray, Schott.

Keetman, Gunild. *Rhythmische Übung,* Schott.

López-Ibor, Sofia. *Blue is the Sea: Music, Dance, & Visual Arts*, Pentatonic Press, 2011.

López-Ibor, Sofia. *¡Quien canta su mal espanta! Singing Drives away Sorrow! Songs, Games, and Dances from Latin America*, Schott, 2006.

My Singing Bird: 150 Folk Songs, ed. Ida Erdei, Faith Knowles, & Denise Bacon, Kodály Center of America, 2002.

Sail Away: 155 American Folk Songs to sing, read, and play, ed. Eleanor Locke, Boosey & Hawkes, 1981.

Steen, Arvida. *Exploring Orff: A Teacher's Guide*, Schott, 1992.

The Real Mother Goose, Checkerboard Press, 1944.

Websites

American Orff Schulwerk Association, http://www.aosa.org.

National Standards for Arts Education, http://artsedge.kennedy-center.org/educators/standards.aspx, 1994.

Purdum, Tim. *Creative Sequence Online*, http://cs.cedarrivermusic.com, Cedar River Music, 2012.

www.ingramcontent.com/pod-product-compliance
Lightning Source LLC
Chambersburg PA
CBHW042024150426
43198CB00002B/61